The Lost Tribes, Are The Teutonic Race: Their Model City Of God Is In America

J. J. Cleveland

THE LOST TRIBES,

ARE THE

TEUTONIC RACE.

THEIR MODEL CITY OF GOD IS
IN AMERICA.

By Rev. J. J. CLEVELAND,

OF THE

CALIFORNIA CONFERENCE.

AUTHOR OF "PROPHETIC DATES."

WITH AN INTRODUCTION BY M. C. BRIGGS, D.D.

PRICE, 25 CENTS.

For sale by J. D. HAMMOND, D.D., 1037 Market Street, San Francisco, Cal.

CONTENTS.

INTRODUCTION.

By M. C. BRIGGS, D.D.

" The Lost Tribes are the Teutonic Race. Their Model City of God is in America."

Such is the title of a book by Rev. J. J. CLEVELAND, A.M. I have just finished the reading of it in manuscript. When the esteemed author did me the honor to ask me to read his work, I felt that the pressure on my time would not permit me to do more than glance at it here and there; but the argument so engaged me that I read every line with an interest which increased to the end. True or false, proved or not proved, the theory is intensely interesting, and the earnest and ingenious manner in which the argument is carried, can not fail to command respect.

I am not, in any special or eminent sense, a student of prophecy. It would ill become me to pronounce with confidence upon such a work without consuming more time in investigation. It has always appeared improbable to me that ten-twelfths of God's chosen people, the seed of Abraham, should have dropped out of being. They must exist somewhere. There are few untraversed portions of the planet, and, as yet, no uncivilized nation or tribe has been discovered bearing the characteristics ascribed to the Ephraim. If the writer of this book has not discovered "the lost tribes," he has made a brave attempt, and furnished matter which no thoughtful person can read without realizing a most stimulating effect upon his own mind.

The quiet and scholarly author became so absorbed in his theme as to pay little attention to the elegancies of style. Like a man on serious business bent, he goes straight to his mark. The results of his studies show a wide course of reading and a labor of love I unhesitatingly commend the volume to intelligent readers of all classes, especially to the members of the great Teutonic family.

II.

A CHOSEN RACE.

There is nothing improbable in the supposition that the captive ten tribes, or portions of them, soon after the dispersion, fled west, to avoid the murderous attacks of the terrible Scythians. The first inroads of these Scythians was B. C. 630. This is not far from the time when it may be supposed the Germans came to the north of Europe.

Mr. Sharon Turner, in his history, affirms that "The emigrating Scythians (he means the Teutonic tribes) crossed the Araxes, passed out of Asia, and invading the Kimmerians suddenly appeared in Europe, in the seventh century before the Christian Era."

The apocryphal book, Esdras (II Esdras, 13–41), informs us that a portion of the ten captive tribes, with a pious intention, started for a residence in lands not yet inhabited. They went west, for they crossed the Euphrates. They were a year and a-half on the way. This was long enough to reach the corners of northwestern Europe.

Tacitus, the great historian, affirms: "I concur in the opinion with those who deem the Germans never to have intermarried with other nations, but to be a race pure, unmixed, and stamped with a distinct character. Hence a family likeness pervades the whole, though their numbers are so great : eyes stern and blue ; ruddy hair ; large bodies, powerful in sudden exertions."

Almost without exception these remarks of the historian were true of the old Hebrew race. A German historian remarks: "The Romans justly considered the German nation as an aboriginal, pure and unmixed race of people. They resembled themselves alone, and like the specifically similar plants of the field, which, springing from a pure seed, and not raised in the hot-bed of a garden, but germinating in the healthy, free, unsheltered soil, do not differ from each other by varieties; so, also, among the thousands of the simple German race, there was but one determined and equal form of body." The above remarks are also true of the ancient Hebrews.

Again Tacitus declares: "Among the Germans good morals effect more than elsewhere good laws." In this respect also the Hebrews, in their prosperity, and the Germans are alike.

Mr. Turner says : "The Anglo-Saxons, Lowland Scotch, Normans, Danes, Norwegians, Swedes, Germans, Dutch, Belgians, Lombards and Franks, have all sprung from that great fountain of the human race which we have distinguished by the terms Scythian (not Scythian), German or Gothic." Again he says: "The ancient languages of these nations prove their ancient affinity, the continuous chronology of their first origin, and their common derivation."

The San Francisco *Chronicle* says: "Every syllable in the purest German can be expressed by the use of the Hebrew characters."

To show that the Teutonic race is a chosen people, we quote from Kohlrausch's history as follows: "This veneration for the female sex in its human dignity, combined with their strongly impressed love of arms, of war and manhood; this noble feature in the German nature which elevates him so highly above the—in other senses so gifted —Romans, shows most clearly that nature had resolved her German son to be the entire man, who by universal cultivation of the human powers, should at some future period produce an age, which as now in its literal and many-sided or multifarious views, should far surpass that of the Greeks and Romans." The same author says again: "Our forefathers * * sought to establish the principle that the foundations of every community should be based on individual good feeling, obedience to the laws, and respect for religion." Again he affirms: "This sublime natural feeling, and this purity of their religious ideas, made them, in after times, better adapted to the reception of Christianity. They were the vessel which God had selected for the pure preservation of his doctrines. For Jews, Greeks and Romans were already enervated by sensuality and vice; they could neither comprehend nor retain the new doctrines."

Still confirming the idea that the Teutonic race is a chosen people, Montesquieu declares: "Scandinavia * * has been the source from whence sprung the liberties of Europe; that is, of almost all the freedom which at present subsists among mankind." Again he says: "Liberty, that lovely thing, was discovered in the wilds of Germany." A Roman poet declares: "Liberty is the German's birthright."

We quote from Motley: "The (Pagan) German in his simplicity, had raised himself to a purer belief than had the sensuous Roman or the superstitious Gaul. He believed in a single, Supreme, Almighty God, *All-Vater* or All-Father. This Divinity was too sublime to be 'incarnated or imaged, too infinite to be enclosed in temples built with hands."

Once more we quote, in reference to the size of the brain, from Morton's "Types of Mankind." The size is given in cubic inches, as follows:

Teutonic Group_____92
Celtic Group_____87
Malays_____85
American Indians_____84
Negroes_____83
Chinese_____82
Indostanees and Egyptians_____80
Hottentots and Australians_____75

This agrees with a passage from a speech by King Agrippa, quoted by Josephus. After speaking of the enormous bodies of the Germans, he says: "They have minds greater than their bodies, and a soul that despises death."

From Kemble's *Saxons in England*, we quote: "We argue only that nations possessing in so pre-eminent a degree as the Germans the principles, the arts and institutions of civilization, must have passed through a long apprenticeship of action and suffering, and have learned in the rough school of practise the wisdom they embodied in their lives."

In this discussion we shall see that these tribes are the protestants, the missionaries, those who observe the Sabbath, the Bible readers, those who zealously promote public instruction, those who break every yoke, those who feed the hungry and clothe the naked, the lovers of freedom, those who are capable of self-government, and the masters on the land and on the sea.

III.

DEATH AND RESURRECTION.

In Deut. xxxii:26–28, the Lord says: " *I said I would scatter* (the lxx reads, 'I will scatter') *them into corners, I would make* (the lxx reads, 'I will make') *the remembrance of them to cease from among men: were it not that I feared* (for 'were it not that I feared' read 'if not, I shall fear'), *the wrath of the enemy, lest their adversaries should behave themselves strangely, and lest they* (the Hebrews) *should say, 'Our hand is high, and the Lord hath not done all this.' For they are a nation void of counsel, neither is there any understanding in them.*"

The idea of the text is, that for a time the people Israel must be hid in order to shield them from the bitter treatment of their enemies. If they had not been hid, it would have given the enemies a chance to insult the Lord and his word, as did the infidel emperor, Julian, when he attempted to build the temple at Jerusalem with its former glory, and to establish again the Jewish ritualistic service, and again to fill the city with unbelieving Jews. The plan was disappointed, for balls of fire came out of the ground, and drove the workmen away. The Lord hid them, also, lest when they came to honor and power they should show much family pride, and forget that He had honored them, and should boast that they did the wonders which the prophets said God would perform. In other words, he hid them lest they should act as the unbelieving Jews have done.

Once the Niagara, the Yo Semite, the Andes, the Rocky Mountains, the Amazon, the Mississippi, and the great prairies, were hid, but having been found there is no probability that they will be lost again. So if we find the scattered tribes, and trace out the glory which the prophet said would attach to them, they will never again pass out of sight. The hiding of the tribes has been done in the corners of northwestern Europe.

Joseph, forced into Egypt and lost to all men, and then rising to kingly dignity in the land, and then becoming its savior, as well as the savior of his father and brethren, is a type of Ephraim or the lost tribes. They also were thrust out of the promised land. They also have been found, because they have shown many kingly traits. They also have been found because they have fulfilled the word of the Lord.

In Rom. ii:15, the apostle says: "*If the casting away of them* (Israel) *be the reconciling of the world, what shall the receiving of them be but life from the dead ?*"

Life from the dead is a resurrection. It is here implied that there shall be a notable resurrection of Israel.

"*For if the first fruit be holy, the lump is also holy; and if the root be holy, so are the branches.*"

From this language we conclude that the Lord has as high a regard for the modern chosen remnant of Israel, as He had for the tribes in the days of Moses and Samuel.

Further, the apostle asserts: "*For I would not, brethren, that ye should be ignorant of this mystery, lest ye should be wise in your own conceits, that blindness in part* (upon a part), *is happened to Israel, until the fullness of the Gentiles*

*be come in; and so all Israel shall be saved: as it is written,
There shall come out of Zion the Deliverer, and shall turn
away ungodliness from Jacob."*

Instead of reading the phrase "that blindness in part
is happened to Israel," it is well to follow Conybeare and
Howson, and read, "that blindness has fallen upon a part
of Israel." Here, as in other portions of the Apostle's
argument, he concludes that rejected Israel will be restored.
The fullness of the Gentiles came in when they ceased to
come to Christ, and turned aside to lies. The fullness of
the Gentiles also came in when the Moslem Arabs on the
one side, and the Teutonic tribes as well as the Huns on
the other, overran two-thirds of the first Christian Empire.
When the Teutonic tribes overpowered the western Roman
Empire, blindness began to depart from them, or they were
converted.

The Lord declares (Matt. xxiv:31): *"And He shall
send His angels with a great sound of a trumpet, and they
shall gather together his elect from the four winds, from one
end of heaven to the other."*

Among these angels are the first four of the seven mentioned in Rev. viii. On more mature reflection we conclude
that they are those who sound their trumpets to assemble
the Germanic tribes to attack the great empire. These
tribes are the elect gathered from the four winds of heaven.
If they were not Hebrews, He would not have termed them
his elect. In Rev. vii:1, four angels are represented as
standing on the four corners of the earth, and they hold
"The four winds of the earth, that the wind should not
blow on the earth, nor on the sea, nor on any tree." Now
another angel comes to them, and says: "Hurt not the
earth, neither the sea, nor the trees, till we have sealed the

servants of our God in their foreheads." The number of
these that were sealed was twelve thousand from each
tribe, or a hundred and forty-four thousand. These were
Israelites or Jews, the first converts to Christ. After this,
he saw "A great multitude, which no man could number,
of all nations and kindreds and people and tongues."
These are the Gentiles brought to Christ, or sealed, before
the conquest by the Teutonic tribes of the empire, or before
the first trumpet. The meaning is that the calamity of
war and conquest shall be warded off from the great
empire, parts of which are here mentioned as the earth, the
sea and the trees, till the completion of the work of gathering the saints. Then the Teutonic tribes shall overcome
the Romans, and in time shall themselves be converted.

The Lord says: "*This generation shall not pass till all
these things be fulfilled.*" By this generation he means the
ruling Roman people. They did not pass away till all
things before mentioned in Matt. xxiv were primarily fulfilled. Especially they did not pass away till the elect, or
the ten tribes, were gathered from the four winds to overwhelm them. (See Prophetic Dates, p. 70.) In this
passage, also, the angels are the godly messengers, who in
a spiritual sense led the ten tribes to Christ.

In the fifteenth of first Cor., the Apostle speaks mainly
of a literal death and resurrection till he shows us a mystery, and then he leaves the literal and treats of the
symbolical life and death, or that of nations. There are
two epochs to which this passage may refer. One is the
downfall of the Christian Roman Empire, A. D. 400, and
the other is that of the Roman Catholic dominion at the
great Reformation. In this work of destruction the chief
agents are the Teutonic tribes.

We shall not all sleep. This refers to the sleep or death of the first Christian Empire. He means that not every part of the empire shall lose civil and religious privileges. He uses the term we, for he is a Roman citizen, and he is deeply interested in his country's welfare.

But we shall all be changed. This means that there shall be a revolution which shall extend over the entire empire. This began with the attack of the northern nations.

Near the downfall of the western empire the Scythians and the Teutonic tribes overran large portions of the eastern empire. Though they did not make permanent conquests, they made great changes. The era of the great reformation was notably a period of revolutions.

In a moment, in the twinkling of an eye. In Rev. viii, the suddenness of this revolution is characterized by a great mountain, burning with fire, cast into the sea, and by a great star falling from Heaven, burning as it were a lamp; and in Rev. xi, by two witnesses rising from the dead.

At the last trump. The last trump properly sounds at this event, for it is the signal of the fall of the last world empire, and then of the same empire revived in the form of the apostate church, or great Babylon.

And the dead shall be raised incorruptible, and we shall be changed. The dead here mentioned are the Teutonic tribes. Till they conquered Rome, they did not enjoy civil and religious life. At the reformation they rose to a higher life. Now the prophecy in Isaiah is fulfilled: "Thy dead men shall live." Also Ezekiel's vision of the valley of dry bones is realized

Death is swallowed up in victory. This is when "This corruptible shall have put on incorruption, and this mortal shall have put on immortality." It is often declared that God's chosen nation shall abide forever. At the fall of Rome, by physical victory these tribes swallowed up death; and also at the reformation, by physical and moral victories, they overcame it.

O, death, where is thy sting? The prophet, Hosea, uses these remarkable words while he is speaking of the life and death of the nation, Ephraim. As the Apostle is also speaking of Ephraim, this quotation must primarily refer to him. And also it refers to the literal death and resurrection.

After two days will he revive us: in the third day he will raise us up, and we shall live in his sight. (HOS. vi:2.) The time of this prophecy is so near the dispersion of the ten tribes that the prophet seems always to keep it in mind. Just preceding the text the Lord says: "For I will be unto Ephraim as a lion, and as a young lion to the house of Judah. I, even I, will tear and go away." Then Ephraim and Judah say: "Come and let us return unto the Lord: for he hath torn and he will heal us; he hath smitten, and he will bind us up." Then follows the text.

As Judah is raised up first, his day is the shorter period of 360 years. The duration of the day is given in section XI. We reckon from the time of the dispersion, or B. C. 720. Near this time Judah also was sadly afflicted. Josephus says: "Senacherib (B. C., 710) made an expedition against him (Hezekiah) with a great army, and took all the cities of the tribes of Judah and Benjamin by force." Two days bring us to the birth of Christ! Then the Lord revived Judah. In the third day began the process of raising up the godly, and in 313 the Christian Empire was established.

As to Ephraim, as his rise was later, his day is a longer period. Two days of a thousand years each bring us to 1280. Near this time the Lord revived his people. Dr· Lyman says: "In this century England improves greatly in civilization, commerce and power." In the next century Wickliffe lived. Of him Macaulay writes: "In the fourteenth century the first and perhaps the greatest of reformers, John Wickliffe, had stirred the public mind to its inmost depths." Reckoning from 1280, in the third day of one thousand years, the Lord raised up the Hebrew Protestant people, and the promise is realized that they shall live in his sight.

If for a day we take the notable day for a nation, or 1260 years, and as usual reckon from the time of the dispersion, two days bring us to 1800! This date is very precious to the lovers of Christian freedom. In a high sense God has revived his people, as such, and they shall live in his sight, for the highly adorned city is the Lamb's wife, and he dwells with her. The year 1800 is also remarkable as the central period for one of the most noted of revivals, whose influence is still spreading.

In Lev. xxvi:27, 28, we have the following: *"And if ye will not for all this hearken unto me, but walk contrary unto me; then will I walk contrary unto you also in fury; and I, even I, will chastise you seven times for your sins."*

Making the usual estimate of a time, the whole duration of seven times is 2520 years. Reckoning from the era of the dispersion as the year when the chastisement began, we come to the year 1800! Here again is manifested the dawn of the day for this race. It is the day of their enfranchisement. In this chapter the threat to chastise Israel seven times for their sins is often repeated. As we have shown here and in Prophetic Dates (page 7), the fulfillment may be diverse.

In Isa. xxvi:15, we have the following: "*Thou hast increased the nation, O Lord, thou hast increased the nation; thou art glorified: thou hast removed it far unto all the ends of the earth. Lord, in trouble have they visited thee: they poured out a prayer when thy chastening was upon them.*"

The prophet speaks of the scattered ten tribes. Their humiliating captivity was recent and fresh in his mind, and it filled him with sadness. It is true that the Lord has increased the nation, or these tribes; that he has been glorified in them; that he has removed them far unto all the ends of the earth, and that in their trouble they came to him and called upon him.

"*Like as a woman with child that draweth near the time of her delivery, is in pain, and crieth out in her pangs; so have we been in thy sight, O Lord !*"

The prophet here refers to the Jews. As he dwells with them, and is of their tribe, he speaks in the first person. He speaks of the great calamities which threaten them, and of their constant lack of success.

"*Thy dead men shall live; together with my dead body shall they arise.*"

Thy dead men are the Lord's elect. They are the lost tribes. They are said to be dead because they are destitute of civil privileges. They shall live, or come to the enjoyment of freedom and political power.

In the phrase, "my dead body," a man stands for a nation. That nation is the Jews. He mentions himself, because it is his own people of whom he writes.

There is another instance (Dan. xii:13) where a prophet stands for his own nation. This is the language: "*But go*

*thou thy way till the end be: for thou shalt rest, and stand in
thy lot at the end of the days."*

Daniel stands for his own nation, the Jews. The
English nation stood in its lot, or rose to great dignity and
power at the end of the days, or about 1695. (See Pro-
phetic Dates, p. 37.) Then one of the noblest of kings, or
William III, led on in the race of glory. We term the
English Daniel's people, from a persuasion that the Jutes,
who in company with the Angles and Saxons overcame
England, are Jews.

On this passage (Isa. xxvi) we quote from Barnes'
Notes: "The figure is one that is common, by which the
loss of privileges and enjoyments, and especially of civil
rights, is represented as *death*. So now we speak of a
man's being dead in law; dead to enjoyment; dead to his
country; spiritually dead; dead in sins. I do not understand this therefore as referring primarily to the
doctrine of the resurrection of the dead, but to the captives
in (Assyria and) Babylon, who were civilly dead, and cut
off by their oppressors from their rights and enjoyments
as a nation.

"*Shall live.* Shall be restored to their country, and be
reinstated in all their rights and immunities as a people
among the nations of the earth. This restoration shall be
as striking as would be the resurrection of the dead from
their graves.

"*Together with my dead body shall they rise.* The words
Together with, are not in the original.   *   *   It may
therefore be rendered *my deceased; my dead*; and will thus be
parallel with the phrase, 'thy dead men,' and is used in the
same sense, in reference to the same species of resurrection.
It is not the language of Isaiah, as if he referred to *his* own

body when it should be dead, but it is the language of the Choir that sings and that speaks in the name of the Jewish people. That people is thus introduced as saying *my* dead, that is, *our* dead, shall rise."

In Hosea xiii:1, the Lord says: "*When Ephraim spake trembling, he exalted himself in Israel; but when he offended in Baal, he died.*"

In the same chapter, still speaking of Ephraim, he exclaims: "*I will ransom them from the power of the grave; I will redeem them from death: O death, I will be thy plagues; O grave, I will be thy destruction.*"

This is like the assertion in this book, i:10, as follows: "In the place where it was said unto them, Ye are not my people, there it shall be said unto them, Ye are the sons of the living God."

This is not alone a natural death and resurrection of a man, but the figurative death and resurrection of the nation Ephraim. (See Prophetic Dates, p. 81.)

The passage in Ezek. xxxvii, is an instructive example of the resurrection of a nation. The bones were very many in an open valley, and they were very dry. But by the power of God they came together, and the sinews and the flesh came up upon them and the skin covered them. But the best of all was, "The breath came into them, and they lived, and stood up upon their feet, an exceeding great army."

The Lord said: "*These bones are the whole house of Israel.*"

The whole house of Israel rose from the dead. After their captivity in Babylon, by the favor of Cyrus the Jews rose. The resurrection of the lost tribes was in A. D. 400.

"*Behold, they say, Our bones are dried, and our hope is lost.*"

So the Jews s..id at the time of their captivity in Babylon. The langu ig : was also appropriate to the ten tribes during their protracted captivity, but after the conquest of the first Christian Empire they spoke triumphant words.

"*Behold, O my people, I will open your graves, and cause you to come up out of your graves, and bring you into the land of Israel.*"

With the Jews this had an early fulfillment. The prophecy will be fully realized when the Teutonic race shall possess Palestine. But the north of Europe and America may be termed the land of Israel. In the fourteenth verse it is said: "And I shall place you in your own land." Before the conquest of the empire the tribes were driven from place to place, but since then, always, they have maintained their own ground, or the land has been their own.

"*And ye shall know that I am the Lord when I have opened your graves, O my people, and brought you up out of your graves.*"

After the successful attack on the empire, the tribes knew God, or they renounced their idolatry, and were converted.

"*And shall put my spirit in you, and ye shall live, and I shall place you in your own land.*"

This manifestation of the spirit began at the day of Pentecost, and it has been enjoyed by the Teutonic race more constantly than by any other people. Since the spirit has been manifested to lost Israel, they have dwelt in their own land.

Some prophecies can be explained only on the supposition that there is for cities, or nations, a birth, a marriage, even a divorce, a death and resurrection, and a hell and heaven. For the same reason that an individual goes to the real hell and heaven, the city or nation goes to the symbolical ones. The symbolical hell and heaven and resurrection strongly confirm the truth of the real.

IV.

ISRAEL IN THE WEST.

The land shadowing with wings, mentioned in Isa. xviii, is beyond the rivers of Ethiopia, or in the West. This western maritime country sent out missionaries to teach great nations, and the consequence was that these nations were converted. In Isa. xli and xlix, there is an address to the isles, which we shall see are in the West. In these addresses there is an evident allusion to the triumphs of the recovered ten tribes, who live in these isles.

The stone described by Daniel, which was cut out of a mountain, and which became a great mountain, and filled the whole earth, and which smote the great image, and completely broke it in pieces, hits it on the feet, and they were the Roman portion, or in the West.

In Isa. xlii:4, it is said: "*The isles shall wait for his law.*" These also are the same Isles of the West. Mention of isles and western Tarshish, is made in Isa. lx:9. It is said that ships of Tarshish shall bring "thy sons," or the children of Israel, from far. In this chapter, also, it is declared: "*Whereas thou hast been forsaken and hated, so that no man went through thee, I will make thee an eternal excellency, a joy of many generations.*" It is a western country that was forsaken and hated, so that no one went through it, and afterwards promised to become an eternal excellency, and a joy of many generations.

The Lord says (Micah, iv:7): "*I will make. her that halted a remnant, and her that was cast far off a strong nation; and the Lord shall reign over them in Mount Zion, from henceforth even forever.*"

Those who halt are they who do not go far away from the land of their fathers ; land they are made a remnant. This prophecy had a fulfillment in the first return of the Jews by the order of Cyrus, and in the blessings which followed, as in the coming of Christ and the preaching of his disciples, and in the building up of the first Christian Empire. But those who were cast far off are the ten tribes, who came to the West, or to the coasts of Europe, and to America. Here and no where else have a strong people risen, with the Lord reigning over them, and under a promise that he will rule forever.

We have this assertion in Isa. xliii:5-6: "*I will bring thy seed from the East, and gather thee from the West: I will say to the North, Give up, and to the South, Keep not back.*"

Here the Lord promises to bring the seed of Israel from the East, and he exhorts the North to come, or to " give up," and the South to " keep not back," but he says: " *I will gather thee from the West.*" This gathering must be taken both in a spiritual and temporal sense.

A familiar passage in Dan. vii:27, is in point, as follows: " *And the kingdom and dominion, and the greatness of the kingdom under the whole heaven shall be given to the people of the saints of the Most High.*"

No where but in the West do the people rule.

In Hos. xi:10, it is said of Ephraim: " *He shall roar*

*like a lion: when he shall roar, then the children shall trem-
ble from the West."*

If we understand the Teutonic race to be Ephraim, the
explanation of this passage is obvious.

From Zeph. iii:10, we quote the following: "*From
beyond the rivers of Ethiopia my suppliants, even the daughter of my dispersed, shall bring mine offering."*

We shall see that to the people in the days of the
prophet, "beyond the rivers of Ethiopia" was in the far
West. We understand that these suppliants, and the
daughter of the Lord's dispersed, are the ten tribes.

Those impressive last words of Jacob and Moses,
abounding in promises to Joseph of great power and wide-
spread dominion, are mostly fulfilled in the West. We
look in the same direction for the New Jerusalem, that
royal and bright city, which is larger and higher and
brighter than was ever seen before.

We quote the noted prophecy found in Zech. x:7–8,
which was given nearly two hundred and fifty years after
the dispersion: "*And they of Ephraim shall be like a mighty
man, and their heart shall rejoice as through wine: yea, their
children shall see it and be glad: their heart shall rejoice in
the Lord. I will hiss for them, and gather them; for I
have redeemed them; and they shall increase as they have
increased."*

Here a mighty man is a mighty nation. We conclude
that this rejoicing of Ephraim, the gladness of their children, the redemption, the gathering, and the notable
increase, all came to pass in Europe and America.

V.

A BLESSING FROM JACOB AND MOSES.

It deserves our attention to consider the blessings promised to the tribe of Joseph in the last words of Jacob and Moses. Each of the sons of Jacob is mentioned, and some of them with distinguished honor. But it is a special favor which is granted to Joseph and his younger son, Ephraim.

The blessing of the deep is promised. This implies that in the number of ships, and in power, and in trade in the great waters, he is to excel. This has been true of the Teutonic tribes for many centuries. On the sea the Vandals were prominent. For a long time the Northmen were most successful navigators. After the reformation, in spite of mighty foes, the Dutch, and lastly the English, have signally triumphed. We shall long cherish the memory of such sea contests as those in which the English overcame first the Spanish and then the French. To have the supremacy on the ocean is a greater benefit than ever, and this race enjoys it. This sea dominion affords great facility in spreading the truth to all nations.

Jacob says of his favorite son: "*The archers have sorely grieved him, and shot at him, and hated him: but his bow abode in strength, and the arms of his hands were made strong by the hands of the mighty God of Jacob.*"

And Moses says of Joseph: *"His glory is like the firstling of his bullock, and his horns are like the horns of unicorns; with them he shall push the people together to the ends of the earth."*

The mention of the bullock brings to our minds the nation familiarly characterized as John Bull. The unicorn seen on the arms of England resembles the animal that Cæsar describes as living in the forests of Germany. The act of "Pushing the people together to the ends of the earth," implies a promise of great and wide-spread authority, such as before the dispersion this tribe never enjoyed. That the bow of Joseph abode in strength, appears from a prophecy in Hosea, xi:10, as follows: "They shall walk after the Lord: he (Ephraim) shall roar like a lion; when he shall roar then the children shall tremble from the West." Long after the dispersion it is said (Zech. x: 7): "And they of Ephraim shall be like a mighty man, and their heart shall rejoice as through wine: yea, their children shall see it and be glad: their heart shall rejoice in the Lord."

The story of the prowess of the Germanic race is full of interest. The first notice we have of their valor was before Christ 113, when the Cimbri and Teutones made an irruption into the Roman Empire. They asked for homes in a more favored climate. The Romans would not hear their request, and they opposed them with the utmost bitterness. The Roman soldiers were then in their prime. But if they had not possessed superior skill in the science of war, and if they had not deluded the more honest and truth-loving Germans with lies, they would have been overwhelmed.

Cæsar says: "Accustomed by degrees to be overmatched and worsted in many engagements, they (the Gauls) do not even compare themselves with the Germans."

At length the Germans, about the year 400 of our era, by their superior valor were able completely to overthrow the Western Roman Empire. It was these tribes who overcame the conquering Huns at Chalons, under Attila, who till then had not known defeat. This repulse of these Scythians was highly favorable to the Christian civilization of Europe.

Again the liberties of Europe were threatened by the incursions of the Arabs. These same unconquerable soldiers, at Tours, under Charles Martel, met and utterly and forever vanquished them.

Then the Moguls, spreading terror everywhere, set out to desolate Europe. According to Gibbon they went away rather than to try the terrible Teutonic arms.

Also the Germans stood like a wall against the fierce Osman Turks, and allowed no encroachment on themselves.

The prowess of the Dutch, the Germans and the Anglo-Saxons in many a fierce contest, shows that they are the true descendants of their Teutonic ancestors.

Jacob, in blessing Joseph, says: " *From thence is the shepherd the stone of Israel.*"

The term Saxon we derive from the Latin word *Saxum*, a rough stone. It may have been given them in the spirit of prophecy, as was that of Peter to the Apostle Simon, to indicate character. It need not surprise us that a prophet should appear among them. Josephus mentions a German who had the spirit of prophecy, and made a remarkable prediction in regard to Agrippa. The Saxons may have got their title while neighbors to the Romans. In Mr. Turner's history, he supposes that they were driven into Europe under their leader, Odin, on account of the wars between Mithridates and the Romans. Or the name may have come from some language kindred to the Latin, as the Sanscrit, from which the word *Saxum* is derived.

The term rough stone, or rock, is a sign of firmness, and of stoutness, and of stability, and of good building material, and of abundance. To show that the Saxons have these qualities, we quote from Judge Shea: "The ruffian reign of the Normans; the subtle and contentious dominion of the Plantagenets; the more subtle and not less cruel of the Tudors; the crafty dynasty of the Stuarts, could not submerge the buoyant energy of a simple and constant-minded race of men."

That they are a good building material, appears from their wonderful success in establishing colonies. De Tocqueville says: "The reason for this success is the freedom allowed in these colonies, foremost among which is New England."

As we have seen, a mountain is the symbol of a kingdom. Modern Zion, or Jerusalem, built on a great and high mountain, is a government, godly, powerful and free, in which the Lord, setting aside kings and a state church, rules himself.

The exclamation in Isa. xl:9: "O Zion, that bringest good tidings, get thee up into the high mountain," shows the great power to which the godly empire shall attain. It is implied that Zion, or Jerusalem, bringing good tidings, is a city enjoying the missionary spirit. Such a city will always get up into the high mountain, or rise to great power, and will be fit to lift up the voice with strength, and to say to the cities of Judah: "Behold your God!"

In Isa. ii:2, we have this remarkable prophecy: "And it shall come to pass in the last days that the mountain of the Lord's house shall be established in the top of the mountains, and shall be exalted above the hills, and all nations shall flow into it." Here not only the greatness of the city of God is pointed out, but also the fact that all nations will flow into it, or copy after it.

The mystery of the stone mentioned by Jacob is illustrated in Dan. ii:1-45. The King of Babylon saw an image representing great empires. The head of gold is Babylon. The breast and arms of silver are the Medes and Persians. The belly and thighs of brass point out the Grecians. The legs of iron, and the feet, part of iron and part of clay, stand for the Romans, first in their strength and then in their feebleness. Now listen to what is said of this stone spoken of by Jacob: Then there was seen a stone cut out of a mountain, without hands, and it " Smote the image upon his feet that were of iron and clay, and brake them to pieces. Then was the iron, the clay, the brass, the silver and the gold, broken to pieces together, and became like the chaff of the summer threshing-floors; and the wind carried them away, that no place was found for them; and the stone that smote the image became a great mountain, and filled the whole earth."

The great mountain filling the whole earth is that free government established by this race in America, which renounces kings, and takes Christ for its Ruler. The models of this government are fast filling the whole earth. De Tocqueville says: "The civilization of New England has been like a beacon lit upon a hill, which, after it has diffused its warmth immediately around it, also tinges the distant horizon with its glow."

When the prophet saw that great city, the Lamb's wife, the holy Jerusalem, which represents America, he was carried away in the spirit to a great and high mountain.

By smiting this image on its feet, the ten Germanic tribes, prominent among which were the Goths, the Vandals and the Anglo-Saxons, utterly destroyed the western Roman Empire. Then its place was occupied by the all-destroying Roman Catholic power. The date of its rise was 606. It fell in pieces in 1870. Its notable period was 1260 years. Since 1870 the Pope has had no temporal authority. It was this race that broke in pieces the Roman Catholic dominion. A mighty agent in this work of destruction on the land and on the sea, was the Germanic arms, from Holland, Sweden, Germany and the British Empire. Also the written and spoken words of a multitude of such redoubtable champions of righteousness sprung from this Teutonic race, as those renowned Saxons, Wickliffe, Luther and Wesley, have mightily aided in breaking it in pieces.

As to the complete destruction of nations, the language of the Lord to the prophet (Jer. li:20), deserves our attention. He says: "Thou (Jacob) art my battle axe and weapons of war: for with thee will I break in pieces the nations, and with thee will I destroy kingdoms: and with thee will I break in pieces the horse and his rider; and with thee will I break in pieces the chariot and his rider."

Jacob and the stone cut out of a mountain do the same work, and they are the same.

So, to the same effect (Isaiah xli:15–16), says of Israel: "Behold, I will make thee a new, sharp threshing instrument, having teeth: thou shalt thresh the mountains, and beat them small, and shalt make the hills as chaff. Thou shalt fan them, and the wind shall carry them away, and the whirlwind shall scatter them."

Here again Israel and the stone cut out of a mountain do the same things, and we conclude that they are the same. The new, sharp threshing instrument having teeth, refers to the new inventions of modern times, especially to the new, warlike weapons, which greatly enlarge the gulph between the civilized and uncivilized nations. In this text mountains and hills are the strong and feeble governments.

The language of Micah (v:8) is in point. He says: "And the remnant of Jacob shall be among the Gentiles, in the midst of many people, as a lion among the beasts of the forest, as a young lion among the flocks of sheep, who, if he go through, both treadeth down and teareth in pieces, and none can deliver."

This description more truly fits the Teutonic race than any other. Several nations, as the Babylonians, Medes and Persians, Greeks, Romans and Turks, for about two hundred years of success, acted the part of a lion, but conquest made them effeminate. They soon became noted cowards. But from the first the Teutonic race has been lion-like. The Swedes, the Danes, the Lowland Scotch, the Germans, and, not the least, the Anglo-Saxons, in their history, have ever been brave like the lion.

On this passage, "*From thence is the Shepherd, the Stone of Israel,*" we remark further: The term shepherd has a reference to Jesus, the great Shepherd, in the days of the ennoblement of the Teutonic tribes, or when in the great reformation they renounced apostate Rome. It also has a reference to Jesus, as he comes in our day to the same race, setting aside kings and state churches, and taking the dominion himself. Now the Lord displays himself specially as the Shepherd, or King of his people.

Among this race the tendency is to dispense with the rule of kings and a state church. In America that has been triumphantly accomplished, and it may soon be done in England.

In the book of Daniel there are instances in which the last kingdom, which is to endure forever and ever, in one place is said to be taken or possessed by the saints of the Most High, and in another place it is said to be the Lord's kingdom. We will quote from Dan. vii:27, a passage which will illustrate this: "And the kingdom and dominion, and the greatness of the kingdom under the whole heaven, shall be given to the people of the saints of the Most High, whose kingdom is an everlasting kingdom, and all dominions shall serve and obey him."

We conclude that the word shepherd not only refers to Christ, but also to a Shepherd people, or to the converted Protestant Israel of this age. They are the Shepherd people, for under him they rule the nations in righteousness. Under Christ they break every yoke, and let the captive go free. Under Christ they feed the hungry and clothe the naked and instruct the ignorant. They are the only people who are carrying the gospel to all nations, and in kindness they will soon bring them to Zion. The Shepherd people are those of whom the Lord says: "I was a-hungered, and ye gave me meat: I was thirsty, and ye gave me drink: I was a stranger, and ye took me in: naked, and ye clothed me: I was sick, and ye visited me: I was in prison, and ye came unto me." They are those people that feed the sheep and that feed the lambs.

The similarity of Christ and his people is clearly pointed out by an apostle, in these words: " We know that when he shall appear we shall be like him; for we shall see

him as he is." Christ, in his address to God the Father,
says (John xvii:22,23): "And the glory which thou gavest
me I have given them: that they may be one, even as we
are one: I in them, and thou in me, that they be made
perfect in one: and that the world may know that thou
hast sent me, and hast loved them as thou hast loved me."

Jacob says to Joseph: "*The blessings of thy father have
prevailed above the blessings of my progenitors unto the utmost
bound of the everlasting hills.*"

Above the blessing of my progenitors, means that it is
superior to the blessing of Abraham to Isaac, and of Isaac
to Jacob. There is no promise like that given to Joseph.
The favor to him is to extend to the utmost bounds of the
everlasting hills. This means that it is to be far-reaching
and world-wide. The supreme authority, both on the land
and on the sea, shall extend everywhere. The enjoyment
of the chief things of the ancient mountains, and of the
precious things of the lasting hills, and of the precious
things of the earth, and the fullness thereof, shall not be
confined to a small country like Palestine, but it shall be
boundless.

Jacob promises to Joseph "*the blessings of the breasts and
of the womb.*" This implies that he shall have a healthful
and a numerous posterity. Jacob said of Ephraim (Gen.
xlviii:19): "His seed shall become a multitude of nations."
At the period of the dispersion this promise had not been
fulfilled.

Near this same time the prophet (Hosea i:10), declares:
"Yet the number of the children of Israel shall be as the
sand of the sea, which cannot be measured nor num-
bered."

Again in Isa. x:22, and in the quotation from it in

Rom. ix:27, it is said in substance: "That thy people, Israel, may become as the sand of the sea, a remnant shall be saved." The tendency of saving a remnant of Israel has been to multiply the race. This has been shown at the great revival epochs, as after the Teutonic conquest of Rome, and under the direction of Wickliffe, Luther and Wesley.

Since the loss of the ten tribes, there has been no other than the Teutonic race that can be called Israel, that has become as the sand of the sea and a multitude of nations.

Many years after the loss of the ten tribes, the Lord says of the men of Ephraim (Zech. x:8): "I will hiss for them, and gather them; for I have redeemed them: and they shall increase as they have increased."

The prophets affirm that Israel shall abide and triumph forever. They also declare that those nations which fight against Israel shall perish. To assure yourself that such peoples have perished, consider the fate of the Assyrians, the Egyptians, the Babylonians, the Medes and Persians, the Greeks, the Romans, the apostate Church, and the Arabs and Turks. But because of their vigor, and of the Hebrew-like purity of the relationship of husband and wife, and of the Hebrew-like strong desire for a numerous posterity, the Teutonic race has rapidly multiplied.

Tacitus declares of the Germans: "The matrimonial bond is, nevertheless, strict and severe among them; nor is there anything in their manners more commendable than this. Almost singly among the barbarians they content themselves with one wife." Again he says: "They live, therefore, fenced around with chastity; corrupted by no seductive spectacles, no convivial incitements."

To show that the race which we think has descended

from Israel has become as the sand of the sea, and a
multitude of nations, we will mention the German nations
which in A. D. 400 first conquered and then mingled with
the people of southern Europe and northern Africa. We
will also refer to the great German Empire, and to the
Dutch, the Swedes and the Danes, and especially we will
refer to the English-speaking Teutons, in England, Scotland, India, Australia, and in North America. These,
with other branches of the race, fulfill the prophecy, and
make a multitude of nations.

Again, Moses says: " *And for the precious fruits brought
forth by the sun, and for the precious things put forth by the
moon, and for the chief things of the ancient mountains, and
for the precious things of the lasting hills, and for the precious things of the earth and fullness thereof.*"

Both the sun and the moon are required to do service
to Joseph. In those lands where modern Israel dwells,
the rays of the sun are beneficent in yielding the choice
products of the earth. And even if they abide in a desert,
their skill and enterprise turn it into a fruitful field and a
pleasant dwelling place. Also this good promise is enjoyed by Israel: "The sun shall not smite thee by day, nor
the moon by night."

The chief things of the ancient mountains, and the
precious things of the lasting hills, are mines, as of silver,
gold, iron, coal and coal oil. The wealth of these mountains and hills is also choice timber, as the cedar, pine, fir
and redwood. He was also to have the precious things of
the earth, and the fullness thereof. It is easy to see to
what the blessing refers. It is the choice fruits, some of
which are new. It is also the useful grain, to which in
modern times we are able to add the excellent Indian corn.

And it is esculent roots, of which some are valuable, new
varieties.

It should be remembered that abundant stores of gold,
silver, iron, coal and coal oil, vast, fertile plains and exten-
sive forests, as choice as the cedars of Lebanon, have been
preserved uncontaminated, and even untouched, specially
for the benefit of this race. No Cortez or Pizarro ever found
the gold of California or Australia, or the silver of Nevada.
In the Lord's providence, this gold and silver have greatly
aided in strengthening England and America. The coal
fields of England and our land, and our coal oil, till
recently, were of no value, but now they are common
household comforts, and they are indispensable in our
manufactures. The grand forests and the fertile plains of
America are of great use now, but a little while ago they
were of no value.

Moses says further: " *And for the good will of him that
dwell in the bush.*"

This is the foundation of all blessings. This good will
to Joseph, and the nations which proceed from him,
though it may be hid for a time, yet it will never cease.
This is election. How diverse is the Lord's treatment of
the nations which proceed from Esau and Moab. This is
reprobation.

VI.

THE BRANCH AND ENSIGN.

ISAIAH XI.

"*Behold, the Lord, the Lord of Hosts, shall lop the bough with terror; and the high ones of stature shall be hewn down, and the haughty shall be humbled. And he shall cut down the thickets of the forest with iron, and Lebanon shall fall by a mighty one.*" (Isa. x:33,34.)

If noted trees represent men of distinction, the cedars of Lebanon stand for the still more exalted men. In contrast with these renowned trees, a mere rod and branch is spoken of as follows:

"*And there shall come forth a rod out of the stem of Jesse, and a Branch shall grow out of his roots.*"

In Isa. liii:2, it is said: "He shall grow up before him as a tender plant, and as a root out of a dry ground: he hath no form nor comeliness; and when we shall see him, there is no beauty that we should desire him."

The humility of Christ's birth, his early employment, his companions, his messengers, and the disgrace of his death, have been an astonishment to many. He is a Branch growing out of the roots of a rod, instead of the stately cedar. But no tree is as renowned as this Branch.

"*And the Spirit of the Lord shall rest upon him.*"

This was illustrated at his baptism, and was shown in

all his words and works.   He showed it in doing the works
and speaking the words of God.

*"The spirit of wisdom and understanding, the spirit of
counsel and might."*

This counsel was seen in his divine words.   His might
was seen in his miracles, and afterward in many acts of
authority in upholding his friends, and in overthrowing
whole nations of his enemies.

*"And he shall not judge after the sight of his eyes, neither
reprove after the hearing of his ears."*

The meaning is that the fair display which the rich and
the powerful often make, and the skill of the orator who
tries to mislead, shall have no power to lead him to pervert
justice.   The judicature of the Protestant nations is un-
speakably superior to all others.

*"But with righteousness shall he judge the poor, and reprove
with equity for the meek of the earth."*

He began his administration by attending to the wants
of the poor.   At length, in his judgment on nations (Matt.
xxv:31–46), when all nations are assembled before him, he
sends away to everlasting punishment those which do not
provide for the spiritual and temporal wants of the poor,
while he favors with everlasting life those which are atten-
tive to them.

*"And he shall smite the earth with the rod of his mouth,
and with the breath of his lips shall he slay the wicked."*

This was the Christ-like mode of the conquest of the
pagan Roman Empire   By the sword of the mouth, more
than by any other weapon, the Protestants of our day are
gaining the victory.   In II Thess. ii:8, the Apostle refers
to the Roman Catholic dominion, which he calls the "man
of sin," and he says of him: " Whom the Lord shall con-

sume with the spirit of his mouth, and shall destroy with the brightness of his coming." So in Rev. ii:16, the Lord threatens to fight his enemies with the sword of his mouth.

"*And righteousness shall be the girdle of his loins, and faithfulness the girdle of his reins.*"

When, the Lord rewards those nations with everlasting life which feed the hungry and clothe the naked, and instruct the ignorant, he will reign over them, and then shall he be adorned with righteousness and faithfulness as a girdle.

"*The wolf also shall dwell with the lamb, and the leopard shall lie down with the kid; and the calf and the young lion and the fatling together; and a little child shall lead them.*"

This sounds like a proclamation of universal and continual peace. Elsewhere in the Word such promises are made. The nature of the wolf-like, lion-like, leopard-like, bear-like and asp-like nations shall be changed, so that they shall be harmless. These shall even be led by a child-like people, such as those that Christ rules. Such fierce and venomous animals are often seen on the arms of nations.

"*They shall not hurt nor destroy in all my holy mountain: for the earth shall be full of the knowledge of the Lord, as the waters cover the sea.*"

This abounding knowledge of the Lord will cause these fierce animals to become innocent. It will cause war and hatred, and selfishness and oppression, to cease.

"*And in that day there shall be a root of Jesse, which shall stand for an ensign of the people; to it shall the Gentiles seek; and his rest shall be glorious.*"

That day may be a nation's day which began with the birth of Christ. We may give a like meaning to the same phrase in the eleventh verse. Even the Gentiles, though they were mighty and intelligent nations, gathered to this despised ensign. These Gentiles were mostly found in the Roman Empire, and were the most powerful and intelligent people then known. The rest here spoken of refers to the triumph of Christ for a thousand years, in the eastern Roman Empire.

"And it shall come to pass in that day that the Lord shall set his hand again, the second time, to recover the remnant of his people, which shall be left, from Assyria, and from Egypt, and from Pathros, and from Cush, and from Elam, and from Shinar, and from Hamath, and from the islands of the sea."

The islands of the sea are the oft-mentioned isles of the Gentiles. All the countries named in this passage are portions of the old world empires, whither the Hebrews by their oppressors had been carried into captivity. The first gathering was by the favor of Cyrus. The recovering of the remnant of his people "a second time," began with the ministry of Christ, and was consummated by his disciples. In the great work at the day of Pentecost, in which three thousand in one day were converted, the places named are not very diverse from those here mentioned. Here the prophecy in part enjoyed a fulfillment.

"And he shall set up an ensign for the nations, and shall assemble the outcasts of Israel, and gather together the dispersed of Judah from the four corners of the earth."

The outcasts of Israel are the ten Teutonic tribes which, about the year A. D. 400, overcame Rome. It is remarkable that this noted race, though once living in Asia, nearly all came to Europe. Also the children of Judah, though by their enemies mostly carried captives into Asia

and Africa, are eight out of nine found in Europe and
America. They do not dwell with the Moslem or the
idolator. They follow the ensign of Christ.

We may remark that the Afghans claim a Hebrew
ancestry. Macaulay remarks of them, as they appear in
India: "To this day they are regarded as the best of all
Sepoys at cold steel; and it was very recently remarked by
one who had enjoyed great opportunities of observation
that the only natives of India to whom the word 'gentle-
men' can with perfect propriety be applied, are to be found
among the Rohillas (Afghans)."

"*The envy also of Ephraim shall depart, and the adversaries of Judah shall be cut off: Ephraim shall not envy
Judah, and Judah shall not vex Ephraim.*"

This envy began with the successor of Solomon, and
was of long continuance. Foremost among the nations to
grant to the Jews the blessing of civil equality, are America
and England.

"*But they shall fly upon the shoulders of the Philistines
toward the West.*"

It may be claimed that the union of Ephraim and Judah
began with the invasion of England by the Saxons, the
Angles and the Jutes. If this theory is true, the Jutes are
the Jews. This derives some support from a droll quotation in Turner's History, from *The Vetus Chronicon Holsa-
tiae*. It is this: "The Jutes and Danes are Jews of the
tribe of Dan." It may be that the Jutes are Jews, and the
Danes are of the tribe of Dan. It is probable that this
union in England is referred to in Hos. i:11, as follows:
"Then shall the children of Judah and the children of
Israel be gathered together, and appoint themselves one
head, and they shall come up out of the land: for great
shall be the day of Jezreel."

They came up out of the land, or they came from Germany. England may appropriately be compared to the broad and fertile plain of Jezreel.

The highway mentioned in the last verse in this chapter is prepared for the remnant which shall be left from Assyria. The first captivity was by the Assyrians, and to Assyria, and was from portions of all the tribes. Josephus says of Sennacherib, the king who succeeded the conqueror of the ten tribes, that he took all the cities of the tribes of Judah and Benjamin. The modern unbelieving Jews were made captive not by the Assyrians, but by the Babylonians.

In the vision of the valley of dry bones (Ezek. xxxvii) the whole house of Israel are represented as rising. This resurrection is to civil as well as to religious life.

By the kindness of Cyrus the faithful Jews, captive in Babylon, together with portions of other tribes, went back to the land of promise, and there rose to political and religious life. Long ago the Jutes, the Angles and Saxons, together with the other Teutonic tribes, enjoyed a resurrection. But rebellion and confirmed unbelief have kept the modern Jews from rising.

In this chapter, also, the prophet is commanded to take one stick, and write on it: "For Judah, and the children of Israel, his companions:" then to take another stick, and write upon it: "For Joseph, the stick of Ephraim, and for all the house of Israel, his companions." These two sticks are made one, and David, or Christ, becomes their king. They together are saved out of all the dwelling places wherein they had sinned. They shall assemble in the land given unto their father, Jacob, where they shall abide forever. The Lord will make a covenant of peace with them, and he will be their God, and they shall be his people.

By the modern, unbelieving Jews, these promises have not been realized. But to some extent they were fulfilled by the Jews, and portions of the other tribes, who, after the captivity in Babylon, returned by the permission of Cyrus to the land of their fathers, and there rose to moral and political life.

But especially this prophecy has been realized by the Anglo-Saxon race. As we understand it, in this race has been consummated the union of the stick that stands "For Judah, and for the children of Israel, his companions," and the stick that stands "For Joseph, the stick of Ephraim, and for all the house of Israel, his companions." This was done in England, by the union of the Jutes and the Angles and Saxons. At this time the prophecy was fulfilled which implies that when the tribes are joined together in their own land, they will become godly. Soon after the tribes conquered England, they were converted.

At the beginning of the career of free America, the process of uniting various tribes began again, and it continues with success.

The prophecy that the land of the fathers shall be possessed by these tribes, yet waits for its fulfillment.

The LXX may be correct in translating shoulders as ships. In other portions of the Word, sails are called wings, and sailing is termed flying. But why should they be called the ships of the Philistines, or active enemies? For a long time the maritime dominion was in the hands of the mighty Roman Catholic nations. Strong hands seized these navies, the invincible Armadas were overcome, and the ships were used for nobler purposes. So this race flies on the ships of the Philistines toward the west. The star of empire moves westward. The mighty nations, France and Spain, were first in North America, but a stronger race has dispossessed them.

"*They shall spoil them of the East together.*"

The history of the high-handed dealings of this race with the Turkish Empire, and with India and China, is a fit commentary on this passage. They together must refer to Judah and Ephraim. This can easily be explained on the supposition that on the invasion of England by the Angles, Saxons and Jutes, there was consummated a promised union of Ephraim and Judah.

"*They shall lay their hand upon Edom and Moab; and the children of Ammon shall obey them.*"

As was predicted (Dan. xi:41), the Turks have not been able to overcome these countries. But the Asmonean princes succeeded, and so did the Eastern Christian Emperors. The promise is distinctly made that this race shall conquer them.

"*And the Lord shall utterly destroy the tongue of the Egyptian Sea.*"

This tongue is the Isthmus of Suez, just now destroyed by the canal. It will be utterly destroyed by joining the Gulf of Akabah with the Mediterranean.

"*And with his mighty wind shall he shake his hand over the river, and shall smite it in the seven streams, and make men go over dry shod.*"

The river is the Nile, with its historical seven mouths. It is smitten by admirable bridges, over which men go dry shod on railroads.

" And there shall be a highway for the remnant of his people which shall be left from Assyria; like as it was to Israel in the day that he came up out of the land of Egypt."

This excellent highway is made because Edom and Moab and the children of Ammon are brought into subjection, and because the river is smitten in its seven streams, and men go over dry shod, and because the tongue of the Egyptian Sea is destroyed. More than this, in all these countries where this race dwells, there are these extraordinary highways, as railroads, which even go over and through mountains, and God's way in the sea, for great ships and steamships. So the way is swift, safe and direct to the land of the fathers. It is interesting to know that the person the Lord raised up like Moses (Deut. xviii:18), goes before the people. The government in that land, as in every city of God, shall be upon his shoulders. He, in concert with the people, will rule.

VII.
THE LAND SHADOWING WITH WINGS.

" Woe to the land shadowing with wings."

The term woe is the same as that which is translated "Ho" in Isa. lv:1. Competent critics so render it here, rightly concluding that the context demands it. The phrase, " Shadowing with wings," implies that it is a country overshadowed with sails of vessels. The entire passage indicates that it is a maritime country which is addressed.

" Which is beyond the rivers of Ethiopia."

This alludes to countries further west than Ethiopia. This country, in the days of the prophet, was the far West. Even in the triumphs of the Persian Empire, the western boundary was Ethiopia. (Esth. i:1).

" That sendeth ambassadors by the sea, even in vessels of bulrushes upon the waters."

The bulrush is the papyrus, much used by the ancients for paper. By tying it in sheaves an indifferent boat was sometimes made, but such boats could never carry swift messengers. The term here rendered vessels, in some places signifies the dishes of the sanctuary, and sometimes weapons of war, but perhaps it never should be rendered ships or boats. The LXX translates it paper epistles. Paper missives or books is doubtless the proper rendering.

The meaning is that these messengers should go to benighted people, taking along with them their sacred books.
They are persons especially from the western nations,
England and America, who in the fear of God go to
oppressed and ignorant peoples, taking with them freedom
and science, and especially the knowledge of the divine
Word. These persons are called swift, because they are
carried by the extremely rapid vehicles of modern times,
and because they feel that their message is of the highest
importance.

" *To a nation scattered and peeled.*"

This may be referred to the negro race. Having but
little enterprise which would impel them to visit other
lands, they have been forcibly scattered that they may be
held in bondage. No other people ever had such a sad
experience. The term peeled refers to the grievous oppression which the African race have suffered while held in
bondage. In speaking of the hard service of the army of
Nebuchadnezzar, in the attempt to take Tyre, the Lord
says (Ezek. xxix:18): " Every head was made bald, and
every shoulder was peeled." The baldness and peeling
the shoulders were caused by continually carrying heavy
burdens. In the same mode the Africans have been
peeled.

" *To a people terrible from their beginning hitherto.*"

The term people is here used. It may refer to more
than one nation. It may refer to nations who till recently
have been aggressive and oppressive, and inclined to per-
secute the godly, but now, from a complete change of
circumstances, they are constrained to receive the swift messengers who bear the Bible. This we refer to the Moslem,
as well as to the Roman Catholic peoples. For many ages

they have been terrible to the good, but they are feared no longer. The prophecy cannot yet fully be applied to Russia.

"*A nation meted out and trodden down.*"

The phrase "meted out," in this connection, evidently implies that the land often changes masters. One oppressor rapidly follows another. The meaning of the expression "trodden down" is obvious enough. The nation which has had many masters, and which has been sadly oppressed, is India. But the swift messengers have gone there with laws, and schools, and railroads, and the gospel, and things are improved.

"*Whose land the rivers have spoiled!*"

In a physical sense the rivers seldom spoil a nation. They are the glory and wealth of nearly every land where they flow. Such are the Jordan, the Euphrates, the Nile, the Ganges, the Tiber, the Thames and the Mississippi. But in a poetic sense there is one notable instance in which the rivers spoil the land. In China and in portions of India, multitudes of people leave the land, and build permanent habitations on the rivers. The valuable authority of the LXX favors this idea. Its translation is: "Whose rivers, like the land, are inhabited."

But China seems to be an exception to other lands, from the fact that its rivers do truly spoil it. We quote from the New York *Sun:* "A gentleman who traveled on the Yellow, or Hoangho river, in January last, told the readers of the *Sun* recently how great a source of trouble that river is to the millions who inhabit the central plain of China. Much the same story was told, nearly a century ago, by Lord Macartney, about this most disorderly river. Nine instances are on record of its making a com-

plete change of course. It has moved its mouth from
south to north over four degrees of latitude, leaving
many sandy wastes and shallow lakes where populous
plains had existed. Western engineers have been much
interested in the question whether these disastrous over-
flows and changes of the river bed can be checked. They
have been convinced for some years of the feasibility of
keeping the river's erratic tendencies within limits, and in
the course of human progress 'China's sorrow' may some
day be robbed of its terrors."

"*All ye inhabitants of the world, and dwellers on the
earth, see ye, when he lifteth up an ensign on the mountains.*"

See the ensign. The mountains are the prominent
Christian governments of modern times. The ensign is
Christ's. Among all the nations without the Bible, this
ensign is attracting much attention. They are called on
to see and admire the work of the Lord among the Protestant nations. In Isa. xi:12, it is said that the Lord "Shall
set up an ensign for the nations," where it is implied that
Ephraim and Judah shall gather in Europe. But this
ensign is for the benighted peoples.

"*And when he bloweth a trumpet, hear ye.*"

Hear the trumpet. This trumpet is blown to call together the people of these lands, or to lead them to Christ
and to Zion.

"*For so the Lord said unto me, I will take my rest, and
I will consider in my dwelling place like* (for like, read when
there is—Rev. Ver.) *a clear heat upon herbs, and like* (for
like, read when there is) *a cloud of dew in the heat of
harvest.*"

At this suitable time the Lord will take his rest.

"*For afore the harvest, when the bud is perfect, and the*

sour grape is ripening in the flower, he shall both cut off the sprigs with pruning hooks, and take away and cut down the branches."

The saying of the Lord in John xv:2, explains this passage: "Every branch in me that beareth not fruit, he taketh away: and, every branch that beareth fruit, he purgeth it, that it may bring forth more fruit."

" They shall be left together unto the fowls of the mountains, and to the beasts of the earth; and the fowls shall summer upon them, and all the beasts of the earth shall winter upon them."

As birds symbolize ships, and mountains strong nations, birds of the mountains summering upon the pruned vines refers to the well known, high-handed oppression of the strong maritime nations over the negro, and in Moslem lands, India and China. Beasts of the earth are feebler tyrants, which do not visit these lands on ships.

" In that time shall the present be brought unto the Lord of hosts of a people scattered and peeled, and from a people terrible from their beginning hitherto; a nation meted out and trodden under foot, whose land the rivers have spoiled, to the place of the name of the Lord of hosts, the Mount Zion."

"In that time," means at the same epoch in which these peoples have the gospel preached to them. Then they shall be converted.

In one instance, that of the Africans, the present is brought "of a people," while in all the others it is "from a people." A reason for this difference is the utter lack of civilization among the negroes. The building from the foundation upward must be a new structure.

The bringing of a present unto the Lord of Hosts of

all these peoples, to the place of the name of the Lord of Hosts, to the Mount Zion, refers to a change from their debasement and slavery to freedom, to a Christian civiliza- tion, and to a government in which the Lord and those who serve him reign.

As this land shadowing with wings sends swift mes- sengers, who cause others so to reform as to make a present to Zion, the land itself must at least take Zion as a model.

This last verse may also be taken in a physical sense. These presents may truly be given to nations eager to represent Mount Zion, as England and America. In this view, the presents of America are choice portions of land from France, Spain, Mexico and Russia.

England's presents are exceedingly numerous from these nations, not the least of which is India herself. Here again the Lord emphatically proclaims that " Godli- ness is profitable unto all things."

VIII.
KEEP SILENCE, ISLANDS.

ISAIAH XLI.

" *Keep silence before me, O islands.*"

The islands are the isles of the Gentiles mentioned in Gen. x:5. They are Asia Minor and the coasts of Europe. It is a country made up of islands and peninsulas.

" *Let the people renew their strength.*"

This refers to the increase of the Christians from the coming of Christ to the era of Constantine.

" *Let them come near; then let them speak: let us come near together to judgment.*"

When the first Christian empire is established they can come near to the throne of the king, but before they were grievously oppressed; now they may speak, but before at the peril of their lives they must keep silence; now they even have the Lord to join with them, and to judge their enemies, but before they had no authority. But to the pagans the command is, " Keep silence before me, O islands."

" *Who raised up the righteous man from the East, called him to his foot, gave the nations before him, and made him rule over kings? He gave them as the dust to his sword, and as driven stubble to his bow.*"

The righteous man is the first Christian government, or

the Eastern Empire.   He is called the man of the East, for
his seat is at Constantinople.   He ruled over kingdoms.
They were given as the dust to his sword, and as the
driven stubble to his bow.   When it is said that he pur-
sued them, and passed safely, even by the way that he had
not gone with his feet, the meaning is that he followed
them beyond the bounds of the empire.

" *Who hath wrought and done it, calling the generations
from the beginning ?*"

By the term beginning, primarily, the starting of the
Christian dispensation is pointed out.

" *I, the Lord, the first, and with the last; I am he.*"

This differs from the expression found in the last
prophecy, where the Lord is represented as building up
and ruling over the city of God.   There he is called "The
first and the last."   This means that the Lord was the
first, for he made all things, and ruled in Eden, and
established Israel, and with Moses, Joshua, and Samuel
ruled over them.   And he is the last, for he came in the
person of Christ to teach men, and to die for them, and to
take up his abode in the holy city, and to rule there.   But
at the establishment of the first Christian empire, he cannot
be said to be the last in the sense that he established that
empire and then reigned there, but he is with the last, in
the sense that he aided the man of the east to get his
authority and to keep it.   In I Thess. iv:16, where the
various times are mentioned in which the Lord shall
descend, in one instance it is said that he shall come with
the voice of the archangel.   In another place (Prophetic
Dates, p. 79) we have shown that this should be referred
to the time of establishing the eastern Christian empire.
Here the Lord does not himself go before and lead his

people to the promised land, but he sends his angel instead. But there is a good time promised when it is said (Isa. ii:17): "And the loftiness of man shall be bowed down, and the haughtiness of men shall be made low; and the Lord alone shall be exalted in that day."

"*The isles saw it and feared.*"

The isles are the pagan nations still inhabiting the isles of the Gentiles. They are full of fear when they see the progress of Christianity. So the carpenter and the goldsmith encouraged each other, and joined hands, and made idols. Thus the prophet shows that a vigorous attempt was made to revive paganism.

"*The ends of the earth were afraid, drew near, and came.*"

The ends of the earth, as may be seen in verse 9, are where the sons of Jacob came from. The northern Teutonic tribes burst in upon the Christian empire from a fear of the incoming Huns and Alans. This is the reason why they were afraid, drew near, and came. Also a fear of the Scythians may have driven them from their former abode in Media.

"*But thou, Israel, art my servant, Jacob, whom I have chosen, the seed of Abraham, my friend: thou whom I have taken from the ends of the earth, and called thee from the chief men thereof, and said unto thee, Thou art my servant; I have chosen thee, and not cast thee away.*"

These sons of Abraham and Jacob are doubtless the lost tribes. They are the Teutonic race that about the year A. D. 400 overcame the western Roman Empire. The choosing here mentioned is the election which the Lord sanctions. It is the election of nations, and not of individuals. The Teutonic race are the chosen people.

Among the chief men here mentioned are the Assyrians, the Medes and Persians, and the Babylonians.

"*Fear thou not; for I am with thee: be not dismayed; for I am thy God: I will strengthen thee; yea, I will help thee; yea, I will uphold thee with the right hand of my righteousness.*"

Here also he is paying attention to this modern Israel· Since they have become Christians, the Lord has strengthened, helped and upheld them, and no other people ever enjoyed such attention.

"*Behold, all they that were incensed against thee shall be vshamed and confounded; they shall be as nothing; and they that strive with thee shall perish. Thou shalt seek them, and shalt not find them, even them that contended with thee: they that war against thee shall be as nothing, and as a thing of naught. For I, the Lord thy God will hold thy right hand, saying unto thee, Fear not; I will help thee.*"

An allusion is here made to the Egyptians, the Assyrians, the pagan Romans, the Moslem Arabs, the Moslem Turks, and then to the Roman Catholics. They all contended with and warred against them, and they all became as nothing, and as a thing of naught. This promise will hold good in the future. Whatever people attack this race, while they are serving the Lord, will not only be overcome in battle, but also they will be destroyed. A similar passage is found in Jer. li:20. Speaking of Israel, the Lord says: "Thou art my battle axe, and weapons of war: for with thee will I break in pieces the nations, and with thee will I destroy kingdoms." Since the year A. D. 400, almost invariably has this race been victorious. And the Lord gives the reason when he says: "Fear not, I will help thee."

The prophet now speaks of a wonderful new, sharp threshing instrument, having teeth. For the explanation of this passage, see page 29.

" When the poor and the needy seek water, and there is none, and their tongue faileth for thirst, I the Lord will hear them, I the God of Israel will not forsake them."

This is a thirst after righteousness, for the word, and for civil and religious freedom. The Huguenots, the founders of the Dutch Republic, the pilgrim fathers, together with all the God-fearing people who came to America, are pre-eminent among those who thirsted, and were gratified.

" I will open rivers in high places, and fountains in the midst of the valleys; I will make the wilderness a pool of water, and the dry land springs of water."

These rivers and fountains and springs are allied to the river of the water of life, mentioned in Rev. xxii. They must be clear as crystal, and proceed out of the throne of God and the Lamb. This water is the symbol of purity, godliness, elevating knowledge and freedom. High places, watered by the rivers, are the prominent governments. The valleys, or the feebler governments, are watered by the fountains. The wilderness and the dry land are all places where, till this water flows, there has been no freedom, or purity, or exalting knowledge. This prophecy is also true in a literal sense.

" I will plant in the wilderness the cedar, the shittah tree, and the myrtle, and the oil tree; I will set in the desert the fir tree, and the pine and the box tree together."

By the usage of the prophets, a noted tree is the symbol of a noted man. In Ps. xcii:12, we read: " The righteous shall flourish like the palm tree: he shall grow like a cedar in Lebanon. Those that be planted in the house of the Lord, shall flourish in the courts of our God." In the wilderness and the desert, or in places where there have been no noted godly men, they shall now abound like the trees of the forest.

"*That they may see, and know, and consider, and under-stand together, that the hand of the Lord hath done this, and the Holy One of Israel hath created it.*"

The causing of the water of life to flow, and the stately trees, or eminent men, to arise, where just now there was a barren waste, is God's own work.

"*Behold, ye are of nothing, and your work of naught: an abomination is he that chooseth you.*"

The prophet now pays attention to another class of people. They are full of pretension, and claim that they have the gift of prophecy, and that they are gods. They seem to coexist with triumphant Israel. They are the enfeebled Moslems and Roman Catholics.

"*I have raised up one from the north, and he shall come: from the rising of the sun shall he call upon my name: and he shall come upon princes as upon mortar, and as the potter treadeth clay.*"

This person from the north is England. His residence is in the north, but from the rising of the sun, or in his abundant eastern possessions, he piously calls on the name of the Lord. The history of this man is that he comes upon princes as upon mortar, and as the potter treads clay. He fashions countries to his will, and it may be said, to his honor, that he uniformly elevates them. Also the Anglo-American man is one who notably comes upon princes as upon mortar, and as the potter treads clay. No other person ever humbled so many princes.

" *Who hath declared from the beginning that we may
know? and beforetime, that we may say, He is righteous?
yea, there is none that showeth, yea, there is none that declar-
eth, yea, there is none that heareth your words.*"

This refers to the votaries of false religions, coexisting
with the Protestant Hebrews in their glory. He asks,
What prophet have you had among you who, like the
Hebrew seers, long ago, uttered predictions which were to
be grandly fulfilled in the distant future? He says, Mention such a prophet, that we may know that he is righteous.
The answer is, No man ever made such predictions. No
one ever heard your prophet's words.

" *The first shall say to Zion, Behold, behold them: and I
will give to Jerusalem one that bringeth good tidings.*"

The first refers to the one first spoken of in this
prophecy, or the eastern Christian man. He is now
enfeebled and degenerate. But on seeing the decisive
action and the high religious character of the Teutonic
race, in astonishment he exclaims, Behold, behold them.
Jerusalem here means the historical city. Good tidings to
Jerusalem must be from messengers who take Christ and
the Christian civilization with them. Or they must be
persons unlike the Greek Christians.

" *For I beheld, and there was no man; even among them,
and there was no counsellor, that, when I asked of them, could
answer a word. Behold, they are all vanity; their works are
nothing: their molten images are wind and confusion.*"

This applies to the degenerate remnant of the first, or
Grecian Church.

IX.
LISTEN, ISLES.

Isaiah xlix.

———

"*Listen, O isles, unto me; and hearken, ye people, from far.*"

The isles are Asia Minor and the coasts of Europe. They are addressed because they are the place where Israel, mentioned in this chapter, shall labor and triumph. The people from far we understand to be the ten tribes, in whom the prophet is ever intensely interested. In his day they abide in Media, but in due time they become prominent actors in the isles of the Gentiles.

"*And he hath made my mouth like a sharp sword; in the shadow of his hand hath he hid me, and made me a polished shaft; in his quiver hath he hid me; and said unto me, Thou art my servant, O Israel, in whom I will be glorified.*"

As is common with the prophets, a man here is made the symbol of a nation. The one here personified as Israel, became Christian, and was victorious in the days of Christ and his apostles, and at length caused godliness to triumph throughout the entire empire. It is very high praise to give to Israel to say that the Lord hath made his mouth as a sharp sword, and hath made him as a polished shaft. But Israel was so eager to learn of the Master as to imitate some of his high qualities. Christ came into the world to make his disciples like him.

The hiding lost Israel in the shadow of the Lord's hand, and in his quiver, agrees with other prophecies. For ages he has not been known as Israel, yet though hid, it has been even by the Lord's hand, and also he has been hid as a weapon in the Lord's quiver, to use against the enemies. This shows that he has been very near the Lord.

"Then I said, I have labored in vain, I have spent my strength for naught, and in vain: yet surely my judgment is with the Lord, and my work (recompense—Rev. Ver.) with my God."

The hard toil amid persecutions, and the slow progress of the work, seem discouraging to Israel, yet he is satisfied by the assurance that God is his Judge, and that he will reward him.

" And now, saith the Lord that formed me from the womb to be his servant, to bring Jacob again to him, Though Israel be not gathered, yet shall I be glorious in the eyes of the Lord, and my God shall be my strength."

These words are full of comfort. The language implies that though God has raised up this person, Christian Israel, to bring Jacob, or the lost tribes, into the Christian fold, yet even if he do not succeed in this, God will honor and strengthen him by allowing him to bring· in the Gentiles. This promise in respect to the Gentiles is as follows:

" And he said, It is a light thing that thou shouldst be my servant to raise up the tribes of Jacob, and to restore the preserved of Israel, I will also give thee for a light to the Gentiles, that thou mayest be my salvation unto the end of the earth."

In other words, the labor of raising up the lost tribes

of Jacob, and of restoring wandering Israel, whom the
Lord has preserved, is not enough. The Lord will also
set up Christian Israel as a light to the Gentiles, and thus
cause him to save men to the end of the earth. Simeon
says of Christ (Luke ii:32): he is " A light to lighten the
Gentiles."

" *Thus saith the Lord, the Redeemer of Israel, and his
Holy One, to him whom man despiseth, to him whom the
nation abhorreth, to a servant of rulers, Kings shall see and
arise, princes also shall worship, because of the Lord that is
faithful, and the Holy One of Israel, and he shall choose
thee.*"

The person here mentioned is Ephraim. By the
common usage, a man stands for a nation. Ephraim is
put for the Teutonic race. They were barbarians, and
hence were despised. They were fierce warriors, and
disposed to make inroads on the nation, or the Romans,
and hence they were abhorred. They were the servants of
princes, because the Roman rulers employed them as soldiers. But a great change takes place. Kings see their
increasing power and dignity, and arise to reverence them,
and they do this because the Lord is faithful to his word,
and because the Holy One of Israel chooses them.

" *Thus saith the Lord, In an acceptable time have I heard
thee, and in a day of salvation have I helped thee: and I will
preserve thee, and give thee for a covenant of the people, to
establish* (raise up) *the earth, to cause to inherit the desolate
heritages.*"

The acceptable time, and the day when the Lord hears
and helps the banished tribes, is when they overcame the
great empire. Also the Lord gives this chosen race, the
banished tribes, as a covenant, or as the LXX renders it, a

testament for the people. They already have been an unspeakable advantage to the nations, and the future is full of promise. To raise up the earth has a reference to exalting the highways, to establishing the mountain of the Lord's house on the top of the mountains, and to causing that the stone cut out of the mountain shall become a great mountain, and fill the whole earth.

To cause to inherit the desolate heritages will be realized, when instead of the thorn there shall come up the fir tree, and instead of the brier shall come up the myrtle tree. Or, superior men will take the place of indifferent ones.

" *That thou mayest say to the prisoners* (them that are bound), *Go forth.*"

" Them that are bound," are the slaves. None like the Teutonic race, and especially the Anglo-Saxons, have been resolute to break their chains. They have said to many in bondage, Go forth.

" *To them that are in darkness, Show yourselves.*"

Those in darkness are they who have not the light of the Bible. This Teutonic race are almost the only modern missionaries. They vigorously say to the benighted, Show yourselves.

" *They shall feed in the ways, and their pastures shall be in all high places.*"

These persons who formerly were slaves, and these who have just received the knowledge of the Bible, shall have their pasture in safe and strong places.

" *They shall not hunger nor thirst; neither shall the heat nor sun smite them: for he that hath mercy on them shall lead them, even by the springs of water shall he guide them.*"

These recent converts shall not hunger nor thirst,
or they shall have the bread and the water of life. The
fact that neither the heat nor sun shall smite them, implies
that kingly tyrants shall not oppress them.

"*And I will make all my mountains a way, and my
highways shall be exalted.*"

These mountains are the Christian governments.
Where permission is given to publish the Word, there the
way will soon be prepared. John the Baptist was successful in this work. The fact that a way is made, also means
that the road is open to all nations which desire to establish the city of God, or to come to Zion. Also in a literal
sense this passage is true. It may apply to the ways which
a Christian people only have developed. These are railroads even over and through mountains, and the paths of
the mighty steam and sailing vessels through the hitherto
trackless ocean, and through ship canals.

"*Behold, these shall come from far: and, lo, these from
the north and from the west; and these from the land of
Sinim.*"

As in verse 1, the people from far are those in the
East. The land of Sinim is Africa. Then they come from
the four quarters of the globe. On the prepared way they
come to the city of God. This means that they are made
Christians, and they establish free and pure governments
as the Lord directs.

"*But Zion said, the Lord hath forsaken me, and my
Lord hath forgotten me.*"

As usual Zion means a temporal and spiritual government of a godly people. When the sons of Zion crucified
their king, she was doomed to destruction. In the year
A. D. 70, she was completely overwhelmed. Then she

exclaimed: "The Lord hath forsaken me." Next the dominion was established in Constantinople, where it remained a thousand years. After the fall of this city, she exclaimed: "My Lord hath forgotten me." The same exclamation was made amid the heavy persecutions of the Waldenses, of the Huguenots, of the Dutch, during their severe disabilities, of England, during the reign of the bloody Mary, and of the Americans, during the revolutionary war. But the constant answer from the Lord to these persons has been:

"*Can a woman forget her sucking child, that she should not have compassion on the son of her womb? yea, they may forget, yet will not I forget thee. Behold, I have graven thee upon the palms of my hands; thy walls are continually before me.*"

These walls are described in Rev. xxi and xxii. There was early a divine plan of the city, as to the place and time and style of its building.

"*Thy children shall make haste.*"

These children are the sons of Jacob. They are making haste in the more advanced portions of Europe, and especially in America.

"*Thy destroyers and they that made thee waste shall go forth of thee.*"

The most distinguished of these destroyers has been modern Babylon. Her sons, with the utmost reluctance, and amidst fiercest wars, left the Protestant countries of Europe, and then of North America. France and Spain sold their lands to the United States, and left. So the Moslem Arabs and Turks must also go forth out of Zion.

"*Lift up thine eyes round about, and behold all these gather themselves together, and come to thee. As I live, saith*

*the Lord, thou shalt surely clothe thee with them all, as with
an ornament, and bind them on thee, as a bride doeth."*

The Hebrew race literally gather together. Those of
Teutonic descent dwell in Europe and America, and so do
eight out of every nine of the Jews. Zion clothes herself
with them all as with an ornament. The ornaments of the
Protestant city of God in Europe, and of the model city in
America, are this chosen race. The Jews prove orna-
mental and useful as they renounce their hatred to Christ.
Were it not for this race, there would be no Zion.

*" For thy waste and thy desolate places, and the land of
thy destruction, shall even now be too narrow by reason of the
inhabitants, and they that swallowed thee up shall be far away.
The children which thou shalt have, after thou hast lost the
other, shall say again in thine ears, The place is too strait for
me: give place to me that I may dwell."*

The waste and desolate places, and the land of Zion's
destruction, are the northern lands, where the tribes have
long had a habitation. Among them are Germany, Holland, England and Scotland. Again and again were they
made waste by powerful persecutors. And those that
swallowed up Zion are far away.

The children of Zion that speak, are the Teutonic sons
of Jacob. The time when they speak is after Zion had lost
the other, or after the fall of Jerusalem and Constantinople.

These children say: "The place is too strait for me.
Give place to me that I may dwell." These men are
crowded. They desire to colonize. They make good
emigrants. They find a congenial atmosphere here in
America, as well as in other colonies. Thither their steps
tend.

"*Then shalt thou say in thine heart, Who hath begotten me these, seeing I have lost my children, and am desolate, a captive, and removing to and fro? and who hath brought up these? Behold, I was left alone; these, where had they been?*"

This is Zion who speaks. She is astonished at the increase of her family. She says: "Who hath begotten me these?" During the triumph of the heathen Romans, and the apostate church, and the Moslems, she saw her children destroyed. She complains that she is desolate and a captive, and removing to and fro. Her removals have been from Jerusalem to Constantinople, to northern Europe, and at last to model Jerusalem, built in America. Zion is surprised to find her own children, the sons of Jacob, hid in the corners of Europe. She had lost sight of them, and had made up her mind that they were destroyed. But now she sees them come forth from the hiding places where the Lord had concealed them. She sees them building up her own walls, and though much surprised, she recognizes them as her own sons.

Now the Lord proceeds and answers Zion's questions, Who hath begotten me these? and who hath brought up these? and where had they been? The answer is as follows:

"*Thus saith the Lord God. Behold, I will lift up mine hand to the Gentiles, and set up my standard to the people, and they shall bring thy sons in their arms, and thy daughters shall be carried upon their shoulders; and kings shall be thy nursing fathers, and their queens thy nursing mothers: they shall bow down to thee with their face toward the earth, and lick up the dust of thy feet; and thou shalt know that I am the Lord: for they shall not be ashamed that wait for me."*

Lifting up the Lord's hand to the Gentiles, and setting up his standard toward the people, implies that they come to him, or they are converted. The sons that are mentioned in this passage are Hebrew nations. We suppose they are the ten northern tribes which attacked the Western Empire. The daughters are the churches which soon arose among these nations. These sons and daughters of Zion were treated with much consideration by the converted Gentiles. They took great pains to convert their conquerors. They seemed to conclude that these tribes were a superior race, and so they were. They carried the sons of Zion, or the Teutonic tribes, in their arms, and the daughters upon their shoulders, to the high enjoyments of the Christian commonwealth.

When the Lord speaks of kings being nursing fathers, and queens nursing mothers, he is still answering the questions which Zion asks: Who hath begotten me these? and, These, where had they been? Soon after the conquest, the Christian Roman princes and princesses intermarried with their conquerors, and these marriages often were the cause of the conversion of the so-called barbarians. In many modes these Christian Gentiles were the nursing fathers and nursing mothers of the rude tribes. As a completely conquered people, they bowed down before their victors, with their face toward the earth, and licked up the dust of their feet. Now God says: "And thou shalt know that I am the Lord." This is the same as to say these tribes shall be converted. And this other saying was realized: "They shall not be ashamed that wait for me." It is said of these tribes, even before their conversion they had high expectations of future greatness. And Zion, desolate, captive, and moving to and fro, never gave up hope.

"*Shall the prey be taken from the mighty, or the lawfu captive delivered? But thus saith the Lord, Even the captives of the mighty shall be taken away, and the prey of the terrible shall be delivered; for I will contend with him that contendeth with thee, and I will save thy children.*"

Zion and her children were in captivity to many mighty nations, but their strength was not sufficient to hold them. The Lord says of these nations:

"*And I will feed them that oppress thee with their own flesh; and they shall be drunken with their own blood, as with sweet wine.*"

The Lord concludes this prophecy as follows:

"*And all flesh shall know that I the Lord am thy Savior and thy Redeemer, the Mighty One of Jacob.*"

Every one shall know the peculiar relationship existing between the Lord and the city of God and the Teutonic tribes.

X.

ARISE, SHINE—A CITY.

ISAIAH LX.

"Arise, shine; for thy light is come, and the glory of the Lord is risen upon thee."

The LXX renders it, Arise, Jerusalem, shine. There is no doubt that it is a city of God which is spoken of in this chapter, as well as in the xxi and xxii of Rev. In prophecy a city means a government, both civil and ecclesiastical.

Our distinguished Senator, Sumner, says (Interoceanic Canal and Monroe Doctrine, p. 106): "But our city can be nothing less than the North American continent, with its gates on all the surrounding seas."

Rutilius (quoted in Turner's History), says: "Rome * * * by imparting to those she conquered a companionship in her rights and laws, made the earth one great, united city."

The city described in the first seven verses of this chapter, is the first Christian government, with its center at Constantinople. It is expected of a city of God that it shall arise and shine, and give light to the world.

"For, behold, the darkness shall cover the earth, and gross darkness the people."

This was notably true at the first publication of the

Gospel, and then the light spread but slowly. But a scene of glory began with the first Christian emperor, and it continued long after. Then the promise was realized: "The Lord shall arise upon thee, and his glory shall be seen upon thee."

"*And the Gentiles shall come to thy light, and kings to the brightness of thy rising.*"

Kings here may be rendered kingdoms. After the conversion of Constantine, whole nations became Christian. According to Mosheim, the authority of the emperor and his successors was one occasion of this great reformation, while another cause was the high character of many Christians, the excellence of the Christian religion itself, and the fact that the Bible was translated and circulated. It agrees with the history of these times that the Gentiles came to this light.

"*Lift up thine eyes round about, and see: all they gather themselves together; they come to thee: thy sons shall come from far.*"

Still the theme is that multitudes come to this commonwealth. It is a pleasing sight. Sons of this city are the Hebrews. They are the ten northern nations. When the Western Empire became Christian, they appeared to receive a new impulse to take possession of it, and in less than a hundred years they succeeded. Speaking of this time, Gibbon says: "The Goths and Germans who enlisted under the standard of Rome revered the cross which glittered at the head of the legions, and their fierce countrymen received at the same time the lessons of faith and humanity."

In Isa. lxvi:19,20, we have an account of the leading of the Gentiles to the truth by the first Hebrew apostles and evangelists. Then mention is made of these converted Gentiles, who lead another band of Hebrews, or the lost tribes, to Jerusalem. We quote:

"And I will set a sign among them, and I will send those that escape of them unto the nations, to Tarshish, Pul and Lud, that draw the bow, to Tubal and Javan, to the isles afar off, that have not heard my fame, neither have seen my glory; and they shall declare my glory among the Gentiles."

Those that escape of them are the first Hebrew Christians, apostles, evangelists, and others who proclaim the truth. They are those who escaped from the calamities which fell on their devoted race and country. The countries mentioned by name in this passage, are the civilized nations in the time of Christ.

The last instruction of Christ to his disciples was: "Go teach all nations." These disciples are mentioned in this verse as those who declared the glory of the Lord among the Gentiles.

We quote further from this chapter: "And they shall bring all your brethren for an offering unto the Lord, out of all nations, upon horses and in chariots, and in litters, and upon mules, and upon swift beasts, to my holy mountain, Jerusalem, saith the Lord, as the children of Israel bring an offering in a clean vessel into the house of the Lord."

Here "your brethren" means the ten lost tribes in northern Europe. They are the brethren of the Christian Hebrews who first published the gospel in the Roman Empire.

Those persons, in this text, who are said to "bring all your brethren for an offering," are Christian Gentiles in

the Roman Empire, which these ten tribes conquered.
These Christian Gentiles were rich. They made every
sacrifice to lead their honored conquerors, the Goths,
Vandals, Saxons, etc., to the high enjoyments and privileges to be found in the city of God. They desired them
to become Christian citizens.

Christ and his disciples went on foot. But these lost
tribes, just now heathen, may ride in chariots and in litters,
and on swift beasts, to the Lord's holy mountain, Jerusalem. Or, they may have the supreme enjoyments of the
godly in this Christian commonwealth. Before Constantine, the Christians were sadly persecuted. There was for
them no city of God.

This passage shows the ease with which the ten Teutonic tribes overcame the western Roman Empire, and
partook of the pleasures of the Christian city. The Lord
so ordered it that they met with no serious opposition.
And when they came into the empire, the Christian
Romans often treated their honored conquerors with
marked courtesy. The advance of Alaric on Rome was
full of triumphs, and he astonished the Romans by his
gentleness. According to Gibbon, Charles V, Emperor of
Germany, though the zealous supporter of the apostate
church, when he took Rome, treated its inhabitants with
much greater severity than Alaric did.

In the reign of Valens, a million of Goths, fearing the
terrible Huns from whom they fled, were peaceably admitted into the Eastern Empire. But the baser nations,
or those that were not the elect, that came into Europe,
were sternly driven back. This was the case with
the Scythian Huns, and the Arabs, and, till a very
late day in the history of the Eastern Empire, with
the fierce and conquering Turks.

" And thy daughters shall be nursed at thy side."

According to the law regarding the prophetic symbols, daughters mean churches. Excellent sons and daughters adorn this city of God. These daughters are nourished at home.

" Because the abundance of the sea shall be converted (turned) unto thee."

The sea is the Mediterranean and its tributaries. Here the prophet refers to all the nations in and around this sea. In the days of the first Christian emperors, here alone was a mighty, populous and civilized empire.

" The forces (wealth) of the Gentiles shall come unto thee."

Above (Ver. 3), it is said that the Gentiles shall come to thy light. This chapter is full of surprises, and here is another. To the old city of God the Gentiles did not bring their wealth. The " wealth of the Gentiles " refers to whatever is valuable among them.

" The multitude of camels shall cover thee, the dromedaries of Midian and Ephah ; all they from Sheba shall come : they shall bring gold and incense ; and they shall show forth the praises of the Lord. All the flocks of Kedar shall be' gathered together unto thee, the rams of Nebaioth shall minister unto thee : they shall come up with acceptance on mine altar, and I will glorify the house of my glory."

It is known that the countries and productions and animals here mentioned, are to be found in the early Christian empire. We conclude that this description refers to the spiritual and temporal wealth of the renowned eastern Christian empire.

" Who are these that fly as a cloud, and as the doves to their windows ?"

The prophet now leaves the first city of God, and proceeds to describe the city in America which is designed as a model for all nations. He does not stop and describe the Protestant city of God in Europe. That government took Constantinople for its model. After the great reformation, the reformers made many improvements. But they scarcely made any changes in the old style governments. They chose to preserve the union of the church and the state. They did not revolt against an hereditary monarchy. There was a world-wide difference between the rulers and the ruled. Costly churches were still made, chiefly for display, to build which required the revenue of princes and the impoverishment of the people. To complete the good work of the reformers, and to furnish a model to all people, and especially to the kindred Teutonic nations, the city of God in the United States was raised up. The prophet, describing the United States, gives information respecting all the new modeled Christian commonwealths of the future.

Bishop Foster says: "America will determine the future of the world." R. W. Emerson says: "America is but another word for opportunity."

In this question in reference to flying like a cloud, and as the doves, we are reminded that, in the Latin, *Columbus* means a dove. Also when the Indians first saw the ships of Columbus, they thought they were large birds, and the sails were their wings.

"*Surely the isles shall wait for me.*"

The isles are those spoken of in Gen. x:5, as the isles of the Gentiles, or the abode of Japhet. This country is mostly in Europe. In another place, the prophet says: "The isles shall wait for his law." Again the prophet says: "But they that wait upon the Lord shall renew their strength; they shall mount up with wings as eagles; they shall run, and not be weary; and they shall walk, and not faint." Then to wait on the Lord ensures power and happiness to the nations.

The conduct of the people in the isles, or the Europeans, should be observed. Since the building up of free institutions in America, they have demanded of their rulers that the lowly shall be exalted, and be made free, and, in general, these rulers have been obliged to grant the demands.

In this passage, the idea is that the isles shall wait for Christ, who, as in America, shall set aside all the kings, and dissolve the union between the church and the state, and shall reign himself. But "first" the ships of Tarshish must bring Zion's sons from far.

"*And the ships of Tarshish first, to bring thy sons from far.*"

In his commentary, Henderson appropriately says: "By Tarshish, there can no longer be any reasonable doubt we are to understand Tartessus, the ancient and celebrated emporium of the Phœnicians, situated between the two mouths of the river Bætis (now Guadalquivir), on the southwestern coast of Spain."

These were called ships of Tarshish at the beginning, because this city was their home port, and afterwards because they were so large and seaworthy as to be fit to ride on the ocean waves. A ship of Tarshish must be built for the ocean. (See I Kings xxii:48.)

The first discoveries in America were made in ships from Spain. Ocean ships brought the sons of the city of God, or the Teutonic races, to America. Among the most

distinguished of these were the Puritans. Here the most
noted lovers of freedom in the world unmolested can enjoy
it. Here they have an atmosphere, mountains, forests,
mines, lakes, rivers, harbors, oceans and plains, suited to
them. This is the first instance on record where a mighty
and a godly nation emigrates to the chosen land on ocean
ships.

"*Their silver and their gold with them.*"

Such a people, with the character and habits which
they bring, and with Christ to rule over them, will surely
become wealthy. Though they live in a parched desert,
streams of water will gush out; and though they live in
the barren lands, they will become fruitful fields, and the
vine and the corn and the cedar of Lebanon will thrive.

But more especially a higher species of riches is spoken
of. It alludes to the high character of these men. With
such a character, they are the men to build up our
superior sacred and secular institutions.

"*Unto the name of the Lord thy God, and to the Holy
One of Israel, because he hath glorified thee.*"

The prophet (Jer. iii:17) says: "They shall call Jerusalem the throne of the Lord; and all the nations shall be
gathered unto it, to the name of the Lord, to Jerusalem."

When it is said that his throne is here, we are left to
infer that he is our king. The Lord rules in this city, and
this is the reason why such multitudes delight to come to
it. The sons of this holy city bring all their precious
treasures to the name of the Lord, and consecrate them to
him, because he hath made the city glorious.

"*And the sons of strangers shall build up thy walls, and
their kings shall minister unto thee.*"

In building a city, erecting the walls is pioneer work.

Nearly the whole of this country was once owned by foreign nations, whose institutions were utterly diverse from ours. These nations were France, Spain, Mexico and Russia. These peoples may well be called strangers. The Dutch and the Swedes also had a part in the settlement. But evidently, by a heavenly plan, all came to form a part of this great union.

It is one of the surprising things mentioned in this prophecy that the kings of these strangers should minister unto us. These kings have always shown an intense hatred to such institutions as ours. They know that republics threaten danger to them. Yet each one of these kings has ministered to us by selling us the very choice portions of our country; by furnishing us multitudes of valuable inhabitants; and France, especially, by helping to fight our battles.

"*For in my wrath I smote thee, but in my favor have I had mercy on thee.*"

The smiting refers to the old time calamities which befel the old city of God, Jerusalem, and Constantinople. And we must utter the monitory truth that the Lord has been angry with even this city, and has chastised it. The favor shown is the modern instances of the Lord's great love to this city.

"*Therefore thy gates shall be open continually; they shall not be shut day nor night; that men may bring unto thee the forces* (wealth—Rev. Ver.) *of the Gentiles, and that their kings may be brought.*"

These gates are more particularly described in Rev. xxi: 13. Here it is said that there are three on each side of a square city. These gates are seaports, that thrive by home and foreign trade. Here is another surprise, that these

gates are kept open continually. In this respect it is
unlike any other city. They are kept open that the forces
of the Gentiles may be brought to it. There is an invitation
to the Gentiles to bring every good thing to this city; but
they must bring nothing that impoverishes, or that causes
the fine gold to become dim. When the Gentiles, or the
Roman Catholics, allow men to bring within the walls of
this city their choicest treasures, or their best citizens, they
are commonly much improved by the removal. The
oppression of the governments of Europe has constantly
constrained multitudes of her noblest people to come to
this land, where the soil and the atmosphere are favorable
to liberty. The absence of unnatural restraint; our free
schools; the fact that our young men are not obliged to
spend many years of their most precious time in military
service; the general invitation to foreigners, not only to
become citizens, but also landholders, may be taken as an
assurance that the gates are open continually.

In this verse the idea is expressed that the gates shall
be open continually, that their kings, or kingdoms, may
be brought. It is here implied that as this government is
by the people and for the people, and as God is the right-
ful King over it, as well as over all Christian lands, there
will be no use for kings or old-fashioned kingdoms.
Kingdoms shall be brought to the city of God, or their
institutions shall conform to those of the great Christian
republic.

"*For the nation and kingdom that will not serve thee shall
perish; yea, those nations shall be utterly wasted.*"

Here the prophet gives a reason why the kings or kingdoms shall be brought to the city of God. If they do not
come to this government, or serve, or follow it, they shall

perish, and be utterly wasted. All attempts to oppress
this nation will react ruinously on the oppressors. The
statesman, Mr. Pitt, during the dark days of our Revolution, used to intimate to the British people that if they did
not cease their oppression of the Americans, they would
overwhelm themselves in ruin. But after our war a better
spirit came to the English nation, even a spirit of kind
regard to the poor, and the consequence has been that she
has had good success in the race for glory and power.

A man builds a house which does not cost a tenth part
as much as his neighbors' houses. Yet it looks better and
is more convenient than theirs, and it is in all respects an
improvement. Thoughtful people, when they build again,
will follow this man's example.

So here is a city built and ornamented like none other.
More than all others it abounds in comforts. None ever
had a superior architect. It is for a model. After this, at
their peril, let the city builders have enough regard to the
wants of mankind to study the fashion of it.

Here is a nation established by God's people, with the
Lord himself for a King. Every nation that will not conform to the regulations of this country shall perish.
Witness the fate of governments most opposed in principles and practice to our own. We will merely allude to
the Roman Catholic tyranny, the Moslem government, and
to monarchical France. They have gone to the pit. See
the upward tendency of those governments most nearly
conforming to America, and especially to those of this
race.

When the Lord says to a nation: "I was a-hungered,
and ye gave me meat: I was thirsty, and ye gave me drink:
I was a stranger, and ye took me in: naked, and ye clothed
me: I was sick, and ye visited me: I was in prison, and ye

came unto me," he says to the same people: " Come, ye blessed of my Father, inherit the kingdom prepared for you from the foundation of the world."

" *The glory of Lebanon shall come unto thee, the fir tree, the pine tree, and the box together, to beautify the place of my sanctuary; and I will make the place of my feet glorious.*"

The glory of the forests of America, not the least of which are those of the Pacific Coast, should be ranked with that of Lebanon. For many centuries these have been kept in reserve for a people with skill to use them, to make the place of the Lord's feet glorious. Many a common man, in building his residence, has used timber as excellent as that used in erecting the palace of Solomon.

But there is a better meaning in the text. Where the people rule, and the Lord is King, the notable men themselves shall be as the fir tree, and the pine and the cedar. The atmosphere promotes greatness.

" *The sons of them that afflicted thee shall come bending unto thee ; and all they that despised thee shall bow themselves down at the soles of thy feet ; and they shall call thee The city of the Lord, The Zion of the Holy One of Israel.*"

The French who helped us during the Revolutionary war, were near relatives of noted persecutors. Mexico and the South American states may be said to be the sons of those who have afflicted us. Indeed, the present relation of all Roman Catholic and Moslem countries to the United States, and other Protestant nations, furnishes a striking commentary on this passage.

They shall call this the Lord's City, and the Zion of the Holy One of Israel, because they see that here are the Lord's people and his throne. Hear what one of the children of France, De Tocqueville, says: " But there is

no country, in the world where the Christian religion
retains a greater influence over the souls of men than in
America, and there can be no greater proof of its utility,
and of its conformity to human nature, than that its
influence is most powerfully felt over the most enlightened
and free nation on the earth." And again: "The Americans combine the notions of Christianity and of liberty so
intimately in their minds, that it is impossible to make
them conceive the one without the other; and with them this
conviction does not spring from that barren, traditionary
faith, which seems to vegetate rather than live in the soul.
* * * Thus religious zeal is perpetually warmed in the
United States by the fires of patriotism."

" *Whereas thou hast been forsaken and hated, so that no
man went through thee, I will make thee an eternal excellency,
a joy of many generations.*"

Before the Europeans came to America, and for some
time after, it was so hated and despised that no man went
through it. What other land is there, now populous and
thriving, and expecting a long duration, that was once so
hated and despised? In this text we may cherish another
of the many assurances of the Word, that the modern city
of God is to abide forever.

" *Thou shalt also suck the milk of the Gentiles, and shalt
suck the breast of kings : and thou shalt know that I, the
Lord, am thy Savior and thy Redeemer, the Mighty One of
Jacob.*"

This is another of the remarkable sayings of this
prophecy. The kings, or the kingdoms, and the Gentiles,
are the fierce enemies of this country, because, unlike
theirs, it has no need of the light of the sun, or of the
moon; or because it is a republic. But these kings and

kingdoms and Gentiles, furnish land for this city, and they fight battles for it, and, what grieves them the most, they furnish people for it, so that in a few years it grows and becomes one of the mightiest empires in the world.

"*For brass I will bring gold, and for iron I will bring silver, and for wood brass, and for stones iron.*"

In II Chron. i:15, it is said: "Solomon made silver and gold at Jerusalem as plenteous as stones, and cedar trees made he as the sycamore trees that are in the vale for abundance." So the modern city of God shall abound in wealth.

Mention is made of this abundance of gold in Rev. xxi: 18, where the city is described as "Pure gold, like unto clear glass." Here the excellence of our institutions, founded on the Bible, and our kingly men, are pointed out. In the governments described by Daniel, in order, the first is gold, the next is silver, then brass, then iron, then iron mixed with clay. But at the last we come back to the purest and most precious gold. This is the golden age.

"*I will also make thy officers peace, and thine exactors righteousness.*"

In this city, where every kingly man is thought capable of ruling himself, the officers are peace. They are peace officers, as the constable and the magistrate. Even the president is called the chief magistrate. Here there is no need of a standing army.

The exactors here mentioned are such as the publicans (tax gatherers). Both among the Jews and the heathen, their oppressions made them odious. Theocritus is quoted as saying: "Among the beasts of the wilderness, bears and lions are the most cruel; among the beasts of the city, the publican and the parasite." The Jews so despised them that they would not accept their offerings in the temple, and they ranked them with sinners and harlots. But our exactors are righteousness.

"*Violence shall no more be heard in thy land, wasting nor destruction within thy borders; but thou shalt call thy walls salvation, and thy gates praise.*"

This foretokens the universal peace so often promised. Violence has been common in the former cities, as in Jerusalem and Constantinople. Here we diligently cultivate the arts of peace, and oblige the lion to eat straw, like the ox. Even in our last great struggle to enforce righteousness, the war was entirely confined to that portion of the land which had revolted. De Tocqueville says: "The conquests of the Americans are, therefore, gained by the plowshare." In this land, as in England, the special reason for freedom from foreign violence, is our high ocean walls, and our inimitable gates of pearl. Let us then call our walls Salvation, and our gates Praise.

"*The sun shall be no more thy light by day; neither for brightness shall the moon give light unto thee: but the Lord shall be unto thee an everlasting light, and thy God thy glory.*"

"Sun" means kingly authority, "moon" means the state church. As the moon depends on the sun for light and gravitation, so the spiritual depends on the temporal authority.

The poets sometimes characterize the king a sun. So Shakespeare makes Wolsey term Henry VIII:

"Seek the king,
That sun, I pray, may never set."

So, again, Shakespeare makes King Saturnius say:

"What, hath the firmament more suns than one ?"

To whom Lucius replies:

"What boots it thee to call thyself a sun?"

From the first it was the design that the government should be as it was in the days of Moses, Joshua and Samuel. Samuel was displeased when the people demanded a king. He desired that the Lord should rule over them. When the people asked Gideon to reign as king, he said: "I will not rule over you, neither shall my son rule over you: the Lord shall rule over you."

The Lord told Samuel to speak as follows to those who desired a king: "This will be the manner of the king that shall reign over you: he will take your sons, and appoint them for himself, for his chariots, and to be his horsemen; and some shall run before his chariots. * * * And he will take the tenth of your seed, and of your vineyards, and give to his officers, and to his servants. And he will take your men servants, and your maid servants, and your goodliest young men, and your asses, and put them to his work. He will take the tenth of your sheep, and ye shall be his servants. And ye shall cry out in that day because of your king which ye shall have chosen you; and the Lord will not hear you in that day."

For many centuries the people have cried out on the account of their chosen kings, and the Lord did not hear, till at the close of the last century a better day arose.

Cromwell once read this passage in Isa. i:26: "And I will restore thy judges as at the first, and thy counsellors as at the beginning: afterward thou shalt be called the city of righteousness, the faithful city," and he thought, at first, that the work would be done in his day. But he was sadly disappointed. Yet in America it is realized. We do not suppose that the Lord would be so strongly against the rule of kings in the days of Samuel, and yet favor them in the days of Washington.

The Lord sa'd to Samuel: "They (the people) have not rejected thee, but they have rejected me, that I should not reign over them." It is the opinion of many wise men that a free government cannot survive, unless the Lord reigns over it. De Tocqueville says: "Despotism may govern without faith, but liberty cannot." Again he says: "And what can be done with a people who are their own masters, if they be not submissive to the Deity?"

Judge Shea says: "If there can be said to be a genius for civil society, which induces more than another towards a republican system of government, it is surely that disposition brought into Britain from the isles of the Elbe, and from the Rhine, by the Jutes, the Angles and the Saxons."

The separation between the church and the state is more fully discussed in Isa. iv:1, in these words: "And in that day seven women shall take hold of one man, saying: We will eat our own bread, and wear our own apparel; only let us be called by thy name, to take away our reproach."

This passage does no service to polygamy, which ever degrades the sexes. God has never ordained it, because he has made as many males as females. Also, where it is practiced, the women never boast that they will eat their own bread and wear their own apparel. This is one of the prophecies which has waited long for its fulfilment. It points out the time when there is a separation between the church and the state. According to the common usage in prophecy, a woman is a church, and a man is a nation. In America, the several Christian denominations do not ask or desire the support of the government. They say, We will eat our own bread, and wear our own apparel. All they ask is that they may be protected, or that they may be called by the nation's name. Give a church protection, and it will secure for itself an ample support. We are favored with a "free church in a free state."

An eminent bishop, after visiting many countries afflicted with this unnatural union, declared that "It is the choicest instrument of the devil to ruin men."

When the Lord sets up his government, he intends that it shall be an everlasting favor. In this passage, he says of this noted city: "The Lord shall be unto thee an everlasting light, and thy God thy glory." One of the high honors bestowed on Christ is that of the title of the everlasting Father. This seems appropriate. Late in the history of the world, when he cometh in the glory of his Father, Christ is the everlasting Father, because he will reign forever."

"*Thy sun shall no more go down; neither shall thy moon withdraw itself: for the Lord shall be thine everlasting light, and the days of thy mourning shall be ended.*"

The meaning is the same as that in Rev.: "And there shall be no night there." Both passages describe the same city. God never will let the old sun and moon shine. He never will withdraw his light; or, he will reign forever.

"And the days of thy mourning shall be ended," and the passage in Rev.: "And there shall be no more curse," are equivalent. They both refer to the same city. This is a good word. No wonder that the people flock to such a place. There are several heavy curses from which the people gladly would be freed. Among these are war, slavery, oppressive taxation, sacerdotal tyranny, and famine of the Word.

" *Thy people also shall be all righteous.*"

The passage in Rev. xxi:27, has a similar meaning, and refers to the same city: " And there shall in no wise enter into it anything that defileth, neither whatsoever worketh abomination, or maketh a lie: but they which are written in the Lamb's book of life."

We shall be aided in interpreting these texts by keeping in mind that men stand for commonwealths. In this model country, it is declared that the various states which compose it shall enjoy excellent Christian institutions. But, indeed, in order to this, the people in general must possess a high character.

Judge Shea says: "Our own government, and the laws which administer it, like those of Alfred the Great, are in every part — legislative, judicial and executive — Christian in nature, form and purpose."

Judge Story says: "There never has been a period in which the common law did not recognize Christianity as lying at its foundations."

" *They shall inherit the land forever, the branch of my planting, the work of my hands, that I may be glorified.*"

These Hebrew Christian nations shall always possess this land as a heritage. This planting is more fully mentioned in the third verse of the next chapter, in these words: "That they might be called trees of righteousness, the planting of the Lord, that he might be glorified." Trees of righteousness are exalted, godly men. Ever dwelling in the land as they do, they glorify God.

" A little one shall become a thousand, and a small one a strong nation: I the Lord will hasten it in his time."

One instance out of many will illustrate this text. In 1847, California was little else than a desolate wilderness. The new spirit which was awakened, by its coming into the possession of this race, made it, in 1850, a great and populous state, of sufficient importance to cause it to be admitted into the union of great states.

XI.
THE NEW JERUSALEM.

" And I saw a new heaven and a new earth: for the first heaven and the first earth were passed away; and there was no more sea."

" Sea " means the benighted Roman Catholics on the Mediterranean. It gives up its dead when the people secure intellectual, spiritual and political life.

He saw a new heaven, or he saw those nations which once had the chief authority obliged to surrender it, while others take their place. He saw a new earth, or he saw the lowly but robust nations in Europe improved, and putting on great authority.

The apostle, Peter, looks forward to that time, when he says (II Pet. iii:10): " But the day of the Lord will come as a thief in the night; in the which the heavens shall pass away with a great noise, and the elements shall melt with fervent heat, the earth also and the works that are therein shall be burned up.", And again, in the same chapter, he uses language like that of John, when he says: " Nevertheless we, according to his promise, look for new heavens and a new earth, wherein dwelleth righteousness."

Carlyle, speaking of the French Revolution, says: " Once, after a thousand years, all nations were to see the great conflagration and self-combustion of a nation, and learn from it if they could."

The language of Macaulay is of like import, as follows: "The Reformation is an event long past. That volcano has spent its rage. The wide waste produced by its outbreak is forgotten. The landmarks which were swept away have been replaced. The ruined edifices have been repaired. The lava has covered with a rich incrustation the fields which it once devastated, and, after having turned a beautiful and fruitful garden into a desert, has again turned the desert into a still more beautiful and fruitful garden. The second great eruption (the French Revolution) is not yet over. The marks of its ravages are still all around us. The ashes are still hot beneath our feet. In some directions, the deluge of fire still continues to spread. Yet experience surely entitles us to believe that this explosion, like that which preceded it, will fertilize the soil which it has devastated."

"*And I John saw the holy city, New Jerusalem, coming down from God out of heaven, prepared as a bride adorned for her husband.*"

Observe that this city is coming down from heaven, or it is going on unto perfection. It seems to be the most advanced people in Europe. Their guide is the Bible. The common law, founded on the Bible, directs them. The people are enjoying increasing freedom. They are causing a separation between the church and the state. They are all the time undermining the throne of the king, and inviting the Lord to rule.

"*And I heard a great voice out of heaven saying, Behold, the tabernacle of God is with men, and he will dwell with them, and they shall be his people, and God himself shall be with them.*"

When the **L**ord dwells among his people, in his tabernacle, we infer that as of old his glory shall be shown, and that oppression shall cease. This is more fully declared in the next verse:

"*And God shall wipe away all tears from their eyes; and there shall be no more death, neither sorrow, nor crying, neither shall there be any more pain: for the former things are passed away.*"

This means that the oppression of kings and priests is passed away. The poor enjoy their rights. There will be no more persecution or slavery. As usual, by the term "death," there is an allusion to nations. To organized bodies there will no longer be any loss of knowledge, and of political and religious power or freedom. And in the place where the suffering has been endured, the triumph shall be seen. Unlike the past, with its dread calamities, there will be no more destruction to this city.

"*And he that sat upon the throne said, Behold, I make all things new.*"

Or, there shall be a complete change, both in the temporal and spiritual economy, and God will dwell among his people.

"*And he said unto me, it is done.*"

Or, this is the consummation, both in the temporal and spiritual powers, sought for by all the good and the wise in the past.

"*I am Alpha and Omega, the beginning and the end.*"

This is nearly equivalent to the saying in Daniel: "And the Ancient of days did sit." He was the beginning in making man, and in placing him in the garden, and in ruling over him there. He was the beginning in establishing and ruling over the people in the promised land, under Moses and Joshua and Samuel. And he is the end in the last dispensation, in coming to the world, in dying for men, in overthrowing all tyranny, and in building up and ornamenting and ruling over his own city, both in Europe and America, and in benighted lands.

"*I will give unto him that is athirst of the fountain of the water of life freely.*"

Here the opportunity is given to drink at the very commencement of the stream. To the people of the city built afterwards, a like invitation is given (Rev. xxii:17), with the exception that no mention is made of the fountain.

"*He that overcometh shall inherit all things* (these things); *and I will be his God, and he shall be my son.*"

Here, again, son is used to denote a nation. So in Hos. xi:1, speaking of Israel, the Lord says: "I called my son out of Egypt." In this text, "He that overcometh" refers to persons spoken of in Matt. xxv. To these nations the King says: "Come, ye blessed of my Father, inherit the kingdom prepared for you from the foundation of the world." And again: "Verily I say unto you, Inasmuch as ye have done it unto one of the least of these my brethren, ye have done it unto me."

Again, "He that overcometh," is the nation addressed in Isa. lviii, as follows: "If thou take away from the midst of thee the yoke, the putting forth of the finger, and speaking vanity; and if thou draw out thy soul to the hungry, and satisfy the afflicted soul; then shall thy light rise in obscurity, and thy darkness be as the noonday, and the Lord shall guide thee continually, and satisfy thy soul in drouth, and make fat thy bones: and thou shalt be like a watered garden, and like a spring of water, whose waters fail not. And they that shall be of thee shall build the old waste places: thou shalt raise up the foundations of many generations; and thou shalt be called, The repairer of breach, The restorer of paths to dwell in."

Such a nation will furnish a race of good missionaries. Where they go they will be efficient in building the old waste places. The New Jerusalem, with its river of water of life, is like a watered garden, whose waters fail not. With the light of God, the darkness of this city is as the noonday. The old wastes are many. Prominent among those countries which in the Word there is a promise of rebuilding, are Egypt, Palestine and Assyria. These builders are rapidly constructing India. Less than a hundred and fifty years ago, it seemed probable that nearly the whole of North America would abide under the dominion of France and Spain, but as these people were not wise master-builders of the old waste places, the Lord left the country to this race.

Again, in this chapter we have the following: "If thou turn away thy foot from the Sabbath, from doing thy pleasure on my holy day; and call the Sabbath a delight, the holy of the Lord, honorable; and shalt honor him, not doing thine own ways, nor finding thine own pleasure, nor speaking thine own words: then shalt thou delight thyself in the Lord; and I will cause thee to ride upon the high places of the earth, and feed thee with the heritage of Jacob thy father: for the mouth of the Lord hath spoken it."

These abundant and excellent rewards of obedience, just mentioned, among which are the favors of building the old wastes, and riding on the high places of the earth, are promised to the sons of Jacob. But the promises are realized by this race, especially by the English-speaking portion of it. This is another intimation of the sameness of these races.

Macaulay says: "I have not the smallest doubt that if we and our ancestors had, during the last three centuries, worked just as hard on Sundays as on week days, we should have been at this moment poorer people, and a less civilized people, than we are; that there would have been less production than there has been; that the wages of the laborer would have been lower than they are, and that some other nation would have been now making cotton and woolen stuffs and cutlery for the whole world."

Montalembert, a French Romanist, in a report to the French Assembly on the Sabbath, says (Obligation of the Sabbath, by J. N. Brown, D. D.): "We shall see the two most powerful and flourishing nations in the world, England and North America, witnessing by their prosperity to the price God himself pays, even in temporal things, to those nations that remain faithful to the first of his laws." In other portions of his report, he places the public profanation of the Sabbath in the first rank of popular dangers and faults, declaring it is like a public profession of atheism, "violating liberty, violating equality before God, and nourishing ignorance, vice and disorder."

A Paris correspondent of the New York *World* writes: "There is no old stonemason, no old shoemaker, no old carpenter, no old painter, no old artisan, in Paris. Medical men say this premature decline is owing, absolutely, to a want of a day of rest once a week. Going to museums, poring over books, amusements of every sort, 'improving the mind,' are equally pernicious as hard work."

Need it be repeated that those nations whose institutions befriend the poor and exalt the lowly; which feed the hungry, not only with their daily food, but especially with the most ennobling knowledge; which give the water of life to the thirsty; and which remember the Sabbath day to keep it holy, are such as ride upon the high places of the earth, and they are fed with the heritage of Jacob, and they shall build the old waste places, and the Lord shall say unto them: "Come, ye blessed of my Father, inherit the kingdom prepared for you from the foundation of the world." Such already are two of the greatest nations of the world, and there is room for others to join in the honorable career.

Unless the civil authority sanctions the observance of the Sabbath, to say nothing about natural food and clothing, the poor cannot be supplied with the bread and the water of life. To such a nation the Lord will say: "Depart from me, ye cursed, into everlasting fire, prepared for the devil and his angels; for I was a-hungered, and ye gave me no meat; I was thirsty, and ye gave me no drink."

Of Totila, one of the first Christian Gothic kings of Italy, Gibbon says: "He often harangued his troops: and it was his constant theme that national vice and ruin are inseparably connected; that victory is the fruit of moral as well as military virtue; and that the prince, and even the people, are responsible for the crimes which they neglect to punish."

In the next verse, mention is made of nations which are on the road to the lake of fire and brimstone.

"*But the fearful; and unbelieving, and the abominable, and murderers, and whoremongers, and sorcerers, and idolaters, and all liars, shall have their part in the lake which burneth with fire and brimstone: which is the second death.*"

The second death is that from which there is no resurrection. But in some cases, after a national death, there follows a resurrection. The "fearful" are the fainthearted. They have no disposition to contend manfully for the right. A nation of cowards cannot thrive.

The next class is the unbelieving, or those who reject Christ and his Word. All such nations hasten to the pit. Again we quote De Tocqueville: "Despotism may govern without faith, but liberty cannot."

The "abominable," according to Lange, "are those who through the working of abomination have made themselves abominable." They, as nations, are making haste to hell.

The nations of murderers are mentioned. They are the bloodthirsty, or such as delight in war. The present tendency is to universal peace. Drunkenness is closely allied to murder. So Dr. Franklin thought when he asked our fathers to spell murder backwards.

"Whoremongers" are the devotees of the great Harlot, or the apostate church. And in a literal sense, they are such as are guilty of lecherous conduct. Such nations are hastening downward.

The Roman Catholics, as well as the heathen, have constantly been guilty of sorcery and idolatry. Sorcery may be used in a symbolical as well as a literal sense, and refers to the practice of poisoning the soul.

And all liars are the last mentioned peoples. According to the statement of the apostle, Paul, a characteristic of the apostate church, or the "Man of Sin," is that of "Speaking lies in hypocrisy." Macaulay says: "English valor and English intelligence have done less to preserve and extend our Oriental Empire than English veracity. * * * No oath which superstition can devise, no hostage, however precious, inspires a hundredth part of the confidence which is produced by the 'yea, yea,' and 'nay, nay,' of a British envoy."

Now the scene changes. An angel comes to the prophet, and says:

"*Come hither, I will show thee the bride, the Lamb's wife.*"

The Lamb's wife is the city of God in America. The joyous days of Moses and Joshua and Samuel have returned.

Light and transparency, clearness as the crystal, precious gems, the water of life, and the tree of life, are emblems of gladness. No city is so well adorned and so joyous. In this respect she is fitted for a bride. The extraordinary clearness of the natural atmosphere of America is a sign of the joyousness of this city. She is joyous in her gates of pearl. She is joyous in her river of water of life, clear as crystal. She is joyous in her transparent streets of gold and walls of jasper. She is joyous in being garnished with all manner of precious stones. She is joyous with perpetual light, the light of God. Especially is she glad in the assurance that the Bridegroom will abide with her forever, and that he will be her sure defense. In 1832, that noted Englishman, Dr. Adam Clarke, writes of America as follows: "I believe your nation to be destined to be the mightiest and happiest nation on the earth."

In Hosea ii:16, it is said: "And it shall be at that day, saith the Lord, that thou shalt call me Ishi (my Husband); and thou shalt call me no more Baali (my Lord). And in the same chapter it is said: "And I will betroth thee unto me forever."

During the dark days of the Republic (Nov. 18, 1862), Secretary Stanton writes to Rev. H. Dyer, as follows: "Believing our national destiny is as immediately in the hands of the Most High as ever were the children of Israel, I am not only undismayed, but full of hope."

"*And he carried me away in the spirit to a great and high mountain, and showed me that great city, the holy Jerusalem, descending out of heaven from God.*"

This city is not the one described in the first eight verses of this chapter. Some things are repeated, which could not properly be done if this city were not a new one. Twice the Lord exclaims: "I am Alpha and Omega." In diverse terms the opportunity is given to drink of the water of life. In diverse terms both are said to be freed from grievous evils. In diverse terms the reprobate outside nations are mentioned, and their punishment described. The one is said to be prepared as a bride adorned for her husband, the other is the bride, the Lamb's wife. God promises to dwell in the one, and he is the King of the other. The last city has the glory of God, and it cannot be seen till the prophet ascends a great and high mountain. There is also this essential difference in the names, that the last is called a great city.

As in verse 2, "descending from God out of heaven," means that the city is improving. The laws of such a city will conform to the will of God. The people will revere the ten commandments; they will elevate the poor, and they will have no king but the Lord.

Judge Shea says: "The common law of England came from the sacred Scriptures, which preach freedom and liberation to all nations. Trial by jury—of Scandinavian origin in the form in which it exists in England; the privilege of the writ of habeas corpus; the village community; international law, the offspring of liberal commerce and practical Christianity, were not only unknown, but alien to the temper of Roman governance."

"Coming down from God out of heaven," means going on to perfection, in the sense that the government descends from the old-style monarchy into the hands of humble men, or of the people. In Rev. xii, the dragon, or the old serpent, which stands for pagan Rome, at first is represented as in heaven. Then, when the Christians rise to power, and take the dragon's place, he is said to be cast out of heaven into the earth.

"*Having the glory of God: and her light was like unto a stone most precious, even like a jasper stone, clear as crystal.*"

It is the highest recommendation of this city that it has the glory of God. The Teutonic nations are characterized as a stone cut out of a mountain. When they become Christian, their light is as a stone most precious, even like a jasper stone, clear as crystal. Often in this bright city things are said to be transparent, or clear as crystal. When the common people direct affairs, all things should be made so plain "that he may run that readeth it."

"*And had a wall great and high, and had twelve gates, and at the gates twelve angels, and names written thereon, which are the names of the twelve tribes of the children of Israel: on the east three gates; on the north three gates; on the south three gates; and on the west three gates.*"

This description aids us in locating the city. In the sixteenth verse, it is said of it that "the length and the breadth and the height of it are equal." This will make the height of the wall 20,000 furlongs. This is the distance from the American to the European seaports. Like the United States, this city faces the four points of the compass.

It is not uncommon to term an ocean a wall. Shake-

speare makes the Duke of Lancaster, in speaking of
England, say:

> " This precious stone set in the silver sea,
>   Which serves it in the office of a wall."

Also he puts these words into the mouth of Lord Hast-
ings:

> " Let us be backed with God, and with the sea,
>   Which he hath given for fence impregnable."

De Tocqueville says: " The Americans have no neighbors, and consequently they have no great wars or financial
crises to dread. They require neither great taxes, nor
large armies, nor great generals; and they have nothing
to fear from a scourge which is more formidable to republics than all these evils combined, namely, military
glory." We repeat Senator Sumner's remark in reference
to the gates of this city: " But our city can be nothing
less than the North American continent, with its *gates on
all the surrounding seas.*" On three sides of this city, the
gates are capacious bays, which in general seem to be the
expansion of the mouths of majestic rivers. The bays and
the rivers greatly promote foreign and domestic trade.
The angels are made great by the commerce of these gates.
Among these angels we may mention Boston, New York,
Philadelphia, Baltimore, Mobile, New Orleans, Galveston,
San Francisco, Portland, and some growing city on Puget
Sound. On the north, these gates are the wonderful
system of lakes, and the angels are such prominent cities
as Buffalo, Cleveland and Chicago.

The foresight of the founder of a town led him to name
a noted city on the coast of California, The Angels.

It is said of these gates that the names of the twelve

tribes of the children of Israel are written on them. When Israel in the wilderness camped in a square, there were three tribes on each side. In the four square city of Eze-kiel, there was on each of the twelve gates the name of a tribe. (Ezek. xlviii:31.) That the city of God also has these names on its gates, confirms the opinion that the twelve tribes dwell in it, and that God's laws, once dear to them, are still their guide.

" *And the wall of the city had twelve foundations, and in them the names of the twelve apostles of the Lamb.*"

The city is built then on the foundation of the apostles. Without this there is no permanency. The twelve foun-dations allude also to the thirteen colonies. After the admission of the apostle, Paul, there were thirteen apostles, and there were thirteen tribes of Israel.

" *And the city lieth four square, and the length is as large as the breadth.*"

The allusion is to square dealing in all public and private affairs. But in truth it is a square country. The towns, counties, states, and even the commonwealth itself, are square. The rule is that the boundary shall be a straight line, and that it shall coincide with the cardinal points of the compass. This is not the rule in any other land. The diagonal distances from "Maine to California," and from Cape Flattery to Cape Sable, are equal. By evidently providential developments, the country, at first far from square, at length assumed a shapely form.

" *And he measured the city with the reed, twelve thousand furlongs.*"

These furlongs must be the measure of one side of the four square city. Using Dr. Arbuthnot's tables (see Wat-son's Dictionary) for the length of a furlong, the twelve thousand furlongs, in round numbers, give the size of this country, Alaska excluded. Here again we are aided in locating the city.

" And he measured the wall thereof a hundred and forty and four cubits, according to the measure of a man, that is, of the angel."

This is making the scene picturesque. It is viewing the wall in another form. It is bringing it down to common dimensions.

" And the building of the wall of it was of jasper."

The eastern jasper is said to be sea green (Dr. Clarke). But the walls are the sea. This color is always delightful. In verse eleven, it is said to be clear as crystal. Thus the ocean walls of this city are well described.

" And the city was pure gold, like unto clear glass."

As gold is the most valuable metal, all things compared to it are the most precious. In the image representing several nations, when Nebuchadnezzar is said to be the head of gold, his superiority to the others may be seen in his faith. This was so strong that at one time he published a decree threatening with the severest punishments those who spoke a word against Jehovah. When he fell into unbelief, the Lord chastised him, and brought him to repent and bless his name, and we may infer that he died in the faith. Cyrus and his successors are also honored by being represented by the precious metal, silver. The Lord sent to Cyrus, by his prophet, a message, and he and the kings of his line provided for the establishing of the Jews in their own land. But the rulers of the other two kingdoms, represented by the baser metals, brass and iron, were noted for their firmly cherished unbelief, which in general fitted them to be the relentless persecutors of God's people. In the great republic, the doctrines and the political institutions are the most perfect, hence the city is said to be pure gold, like unto clear glass. Nebuchadnezzar was the head of gold, but this city itself is pure gold. This distinction is made because our city has not merely one person fit to rule, but it has a multitude of kingly men, and they are adorned with the spirit of Christ. Here the people rule.

In the twenty-first verse, it is said that "The street of the city was pure gold, as it were transparent glass." In walking on such a transparent street, the common men who direct affairs need not stumble. "The wayfaring men, though fools, shall not err therein." The transparent gold of the street refers to certain imperishable, precious and beautiful things, which characterize the city. Among these things are the common law, founded on the Bible, our system of public instruction, which also looks to God's Word for its support, and our constitution, which gives freedom and equality to all. It is by the fruit of the Spirit that the pure gold, like unto clear glass, is produced. This fruit is love, joy, peace, long suffering, gentleness, goodness, faith, meekness and temperance. This is the righteousness which exalteth a nation.

"*And the foundations of the wall of the city were garnished with all manner of precious stones. The first foundation was jasper,*" etc.

It is thought that the precious stones here mentioned are a translation of the Hebrew names of those on the breast-plate of the high priest, on which were engraved the name of each one of the twelve tribes of Israel. This is another proof that the lost tribes and our race are the same. It may be claimed that the reason why the jasper is so prominently mentioned is that it is the stone which stands for Joseph.

Brave men, like Israelites, make a good foundation for the wall of a city. An ambassador visiting Sparta, remarked to King Agesalaus that it was strange that the cities of the country had no walls. The king declared that there were walls, and promised to show them. He brought him to his army in full array. "There," said he, "thou beholdest the walls of Sparta—ten thousand men, and every man a brick." Josephus says that these Spartans claimed to be the sons of Abraham.

"*And the twelve gates were twelve pearls; every several gate was of one pearl.*"

If the gates are harbors, the pearls answer to the appearance of their waters.

"*And I saw no temple therein; for the Lord God Almighty and the Lamb are the temple of it.*"

Christ, speaking of himself, said: "In this place is one greater than the temple." In those countries where there is a union of the church and the state, princely prelates, rich and ostentatious, may be said to perform a temple service. So in the apostate church the clergy even claim to be priests, and to offer sacrifices. They also do the temple service. Such churches will have costly cathedrals, intended chiefly for display, and whose expenses impoverish the people. The reason why there is no temple in this city, is that the Lord God Almighty and the Lamb are the temple of it.

"*And the city had no need of the sun, neither of the moon, to shine in it: for the glory of God did lighten it, and the Lamb is the light thereof.*"

As we have seen (p. 82), the statement that the city did not need the sun or the moon, means that kings and a state church are not wanted. Moses and Joshua and Samuel would also say: "If God and the Lamb are the light of the city, there is no need of kings and prelates."

"And the nations of them which are saved shall walk in the light of it: and the kings of the earth do bring their glory and honor into it."

So great is the light of this city, with its transparent jasper and gold, and with the glory of God and the Lamb, that it is said that "The nations of them that are saved shall walk in the light of it." The eyes of the world are directed to this country. The oppressed and the poor look hither in hope.

The kings bring their glory and honor hither, when their best subjects come. Also the nations coming to Zion, and bringing their glory and honor into it, means that they come to Christ, and model their institutions after those of the city of God. The divine plan is to set up a model city, and then call other peoples to walk in its light, or to establish governments like it.

"And the gates of it shall not be shut at all by day : for there shall be no night there."

One reason why the gates are open is that commerce may be active, and that literally a useful people may come in. But a higher reason is that there may be an interchange of Christian sentiments, and that the nations, as such, may draw near. Coming into this city, is used in the sense of conforming. The nations come to Zion, for they promote freedom and equality, and the people are devout, and have authority, and God rules.

In verse 27, the Lord shows what shall not enter into the city, as follows:

" And there shall in no wise enter into it anything that defileth, neither whatsoever worketh abomination or maketh a lie; but they which are written in the Lamb's book of life."

Much effort has been made to corrupt the pure gold, and to make the city other than four square, and to pollute the river of the water of life, and to bring in other rulers than the Lord. Speaking lies in hypocrisy, is a characteristic of the apostate church. How often has that church tried to destroy our public school system, and to prevent the circulation of the Word, but without success. How often in vain has the infidel raised his hand against our most cherished institutions. When the light of God and of the Lamb are in the city, the systems of darkness cannot prevail.

We quote from Macaulay: "The truth is, that every man is, to a great extent, the creature of the age. It is to no purpose that he resists the influence which the vast mass, in which he is an atom, must exercise on him. He may try to be a man of the tenth century, but he cannot. Whether he will or no, he must be a man of the nineteenth century. He shares in the motion of the moral as well as in that of the physical world. He can no more be as intolerant as he would have been in the age of the Tudors, than he can stand in the evening exactly where he stood in the morning. The globe goes round from west to east, and he must go round with it."

Darwin is said to have been surprised to find that the lowest of the race, the Australians, when educated in London, spoke and acted like the English.

" And he showed me a pure river of water of life, clear as crystal, proceeding out of the throne of God and of the Lamb."

The baptism by water is a sign of the pouring out of the Holy Spirit. Christ says (John vii:37–39): "If any man thirst, let him come unto me, and drink. He that believeth on me, as the Scripture hath said, out of his belly shall flow rivers of living water. But this spake he of the Spirit, which they that believe on him should receive: for the Holy Ghost was not yet given; because that Jesus was not yet glorified." Again the Lord says (John iv:14): "But whosoever drinketh of the water that I shall give him shall never thirst; but the water that I shall give him shall be in him a well of water springing up into everlasting life."

In this passage, though this river is spiritual, there may also be a literal allusion to our "Father of Waters." Doubtless if the ancient prophets lived in America, they would often refer to our wonderful natural objects to illustrate religious things. Why not use our rivers as well as Jordan, our mountains as well as Tabor and Hermon and Lebanon, our seas as well as the Great Sea, our plains as well as Jezreel, and especially our city of God as well as Jerusalem ?

This river proceeds out of the throne of God and the Lamb. Our great rivers flow from the cloud-capped mountains. And the Lord makes the clouds his chariots. The prophet, John, says: "Lo, he cometh in the clouds." On Horeb, he abode in a cloud, with the thunder and the lightning. His voice is the thunder, and his countenance is like the lightning. He dwells in the cloud, because he is a God who hideth himself.

It is said of the tree of life that it was in the midst of the street of the city, and on either side of the river. This leads to the opinion that the river runs through the middle

of the city. This is true of our commonwealth, and it is
not true of any other great and godly city. As our rivers
flow through the gates, or bays, they may be called streets.
Indeed, they are wonderful thoroughfares.

He who drinks of this river will enjoy the blessing of purity. It is a pure river, and clear as crystal.
Also he who drinks of it will enjoy the favor of godliness, for it flows from the throne of God and the Lamb.
Also he who drinks of it will be favored with great
joy and animation, for it is the water of life. It is
a sign of peace. Jerusalem is a vision of peace, and its
peace will flow like a river. This river fulfills the word in
Amos v:24: "Let judgment run down as waters, and
righteousness as a mighty stream." A river implies abundance and continuance. Then here the blessings of purity,
life, joy and peace, shall abide and abound.

If our natural rivers should cease to flow, there would
be no more life. So if the river of the water of life should
dry up, the commonwealth would perish. There would
be no trees of righteousness, and no tree of life. Instead
of the myrtle tree would come up the brier.

The Psalmist says: "There is a river the streams where-
of shall make glad the city of God, the holy place of the
tabernacles of the Most High. God is in the midst of her;
she shall not be moved. God shall help her, and that
right early." (For right early, read, When the morning
appeareth.)

Here is an obvious reference to our city, with its majestic river and branches. The phrase "when the morning
appeareth," alludes to the morning of the great day for
nations. Of this we will speak on page 111. The morning, or the nation's six o'clock, began in 1800. Then the

Lord helped this great American city by taking up his abode here, and ruling with his people. 1800 is the era of the rise of republics.

In a temporal sense, the streams, or branches, make glad the city of God. De Tocqueville says: " The valley of the Mississippi is, upon the whole, the most magnificent dwelling place prepared by God for man's abode."

While on the subject of the prophetic rivers, we will mention that one which will be caused to flow near the old city, Jerusalem. We quote from Isa. xxvii:12: " The Lord shall beat off from the channel of (omit of) the river unto the stream of Egypt." River is the object of the verb beat off. Something is beaten off, and the most natural thing is a river. The term rendered channel, is the noted word, *Shibboleth*, or river. It also means an ear of corn. As we beat off from the ear of corn the grain, so the Lord will beat off from the channel (Jordan) the river unto the stream of Egypt. The surprising statement is made that the waters of the Jordan, which at its mouth is 1300 feet below the waters of Egypt, shall be made to join them. Some plans are already made to construct this canal through Palestine, from the Mediterranean to the Gulf of Akabah. It will pass within a few miles of Jerusalem. What would Solomon have thought of that!

In the next verse the prophet says: " And it shall come to pass in that day that the great trumpet shall be blown, and they shall come which were ready to perish in the land of Assyria, and the outcasts in the land of Egypt, and shall worship the Lord in the holy mount at Jerusalem."

This language may signify that when this canal is built, the descendants of the ten tribes that were carried to Assyria, and of the tribes that under Moses fled out of Egypt, shall obey the Lord's summons, and go to and dwell and worship in Jerusalem.

The prophet, Ezekiel, also alludes to this same canal. There were waters at Jerusalem so deep that a person could not pass over them. The stagnant Dead Sea is now called living waters. For the first time, the fishermen spread their nets on its banks. They find a place for them on the opposite shore, at Engedi and Eneglaim. Fish never had been seen in the Dead Sea, but now they are caught in abundance, and they are such as are to be found in the Mediterranean.

It is stated (Isa. xxxiii:21): "But there (at Jerusalem) the glorious Lord will be unto us a place of broad rivers and streams; wherein shall go no galley with oars, neither shall gallant ship pass thereby."

This may primarily refer to the historic Jerusalem, when near it the proposed canal shall be built, connecting the two seas. It also refers to our notable rivers. We are a peace-loving people, and warlike vessels, either our own or those of our enemies, do not frequent our rivers. Galleys with oars are degrading to the oarsmen, and the commanders often are tyrants. Steamboats are better than galleys with oars.

"In the midst of the street of it, and on either side of the river, was there the tree of life, which bare twelve manner of fruits, and yielded her fruit every month : and the leaves of the tree were for the healing of the nations."

The tree of life is the church of Christ. For picturesque effect, it is placed on both sides of the river, but it is the same tree. The propriety of calling this the tree of life, may be seen from the fact that without the church the nation would die. The tree bearing twelve manner of fruits, refers to the twelve evangelical denominations living in this city. This is peculiar to the New Jerusalem, and helps to locate it. The yielding fruit every month, points to the Christian periodical literature, and to the periodical service in the churches, and to the instruction in exalting science in the schools. The leaves of the tree healing the nations, remind us that the church saves the untutored peoples. These leaves are for medicine. They may be bitter to the taste, but they are salutary.

The wise man says: "She (wisdom) is a tree of life to them that lay hold upon her." But the church may stand for wisdom. Again he says: "But when the desire cometh, it is a tree of life." In the church in America, the desire of all the good has come. Also he remarks: "A wholesome tongue is a tree of life." Especially does the church of Christ furnish the wholesome tongue.

"*And there shall be no more curse: but the throne of God and of the Lamb shall be in it ; and his servants shall serve him.*"

The fact that the throne of God and of the Lamb is in the city, and that his servants serve him, is a sufficient reason for the removal of every curse. God and his servants who serve him removed the curse of slavery. God and his servants who serve him will cause to cease the curse of ungodliness, war and drunkenness. While God's throne is here, and his servants serve him, no harm can befall us.

"*And they shall see his face, and his name shall be in their foreheads.*"

This is not literally looking on him, any more than that his name is literally written in their foreheads. Hiding his face is opposed to seeing his face. Like the Psalmist, when we pray: "Hide not thy face from us," we ask for great mercies indeed. But we do not ask for a physical display of Christ's presence.

The Lord said to his disciples: "I tell you the truth; it is expedient for you that I go away, for if I go not away, the Comforter will not come." Before the Comforter came, only one at a time could have an audience with Christ. Now, his chosen followers are many millions, and all are extremely eager to speak with him every day, and by the Comforter, they are satisfied. The advanced church must not desire to go back to the rudiments.

" And there shall be no night there; and they need no candle, neither light of the sun; for the Lord God giveth them light : and they shall reign forever and ever."

A nation's day is a varying period. It may be a year, 360 years, 1000 years, and 1260 years. A night is also 1260 years. For the period of a watch, on mature consideration, we prefer the round numbers, 300 years, rather than the more exact 315 years. In Mark xiii:35, we have an intimation that the Master will come in the evening, at midnight, at the cock-crowing, and in the morning.

With one exception, during a whole period of a day and a night, made up of eight watches of three hundred years, each, every watch is a separate and distinct epoch. This period begins B. C. 600. This is six in the morning, the era of the beginning of the first world empire under Nebuchadnezzar.

Nine in the morning (nearly B. C. 300), is the period of the triumphs of the Greeks. This is the first time that a European nation secures the dominion of the world.

High noon is marked by the advent of Christ. This is the most noted of all dates.

Three P. M. marks the important date (A. D. 300) of the rise of the first Christian government, under Constantine.

Six P. M. (A. D. 600) indicates the advent of those tyrants, the Roman Catholics and the Moslem Arabs.

Passing nine P. M. (A. D. 900), we come to twelve, or midnight (A. D. 1200). This time introduces the inquisition, and the most prolonged and fiercest of the persecutions. It also points out the era of the Turkish triumphs over the eastern Christian Empire.

Three A. M., or cock-crowing (A. D. 1500), is the period of Luther and the Reformation.

Six A. M. (A. D. 1800) is early in the morning. This is when the Lord promises to help his city (Ps. xlvi:4), which, as we have seen, is in America. It is when Christ joins with those who serve him to set aside lordly potentates, and to rule instead. The year 1800, also, will ever be memorable as the central period of the mighty work of God begun by Wesley.

From six P. M. to cock-crowing was the night of the world. But in the city of God there shall be no night. The promise that they shall reign forever and ever, is of nearly the same import as that in Rev. xxi:4: "And there shall be no more death." This language implies that the fine gold will never become dim. The fact that God and his people shall reign forever and ever, assures us that kings and prelates will never *permanently* practice on us their hateful oppressions. The rule for the city will ever be: "The Lord God giveth them light: and they shall reign forever and ever." Like Capernaum, this city is "exalted unto heaven," but it shall never be "brought down to hell." Because it is exalted unto heaven, we must not mistake, and conclude that it is heaven.

" *He that is unjust, let him be unjust still:* * * * *and he that is holy, let him be holy still.*"

These are proper sentiments when nations are rewarded and punished; and they are also obviously proper when, after death, individuals are judged.

" *And behold, I come quickly; and my reward is with me, to give every man according as his work shall be.*"

Often has the Lord come to reward his servants and to punish his enemies, and in this work he has not delayed. He also will come quickly to complete his work as the Prince of Peace, and to put all his enemies under his feet.

In reference to the coming of the Lord, we quote from Isa. ix:6: "His name shall be called Wonderful, Counsellor, The mighty God, The everlasting Father, The Prince of Peace."

This prophecy represents the Lord in various characters, as he successively appeared on the earth. He could be characterized as Wonderful when he did many wonderful works, or miracles, among which was his rising from the dead and ascending on high. He revealed himself as a Counsellor when he came as the Holy Spirit to lead men into all truth. As the mighty God he appeared when he came in judgment on the Jews who had rejected him, and then on the Gentile Christians who had revolted from him. The manifestation as the everlasting Father, is after he has raised Israel, or the lost tribes, to high honor. Then as a Father he rules with them. This is when the Ancient of Days sits, and judgment is given to the saints of the Most High. His advent as the Prince of Peace will be in Jerusalem, which is a vision of peace. In this high-walled, four square, adorned and bright city, the people cultivate the arts of peace. In the next verse, the encouraging statement is made: "Of the increase of his government and peace, there shall be no end."

"*For without are dogs, and sorcerers, and whoremongers, and murderers, and idolaters, and whosoever loveth and maketh a lie.*"

These are like the vices spoken of in this book, xxi:8. To be free from them, people must walk on the streets of gold, eat of the fruit of the tree of life, and drink of the water of life. These sins are an evidence of impurity and ungodliness. They are those which doom a person to hell, and what consigns an individual to that place will send a nation there also. In this text, the prophet is speaking not only of persons, but also of organized bodies, as churches and nations.

When the prophet speaks of persons who are without, he means such as abide in other lands, or, at least, they are trained elsewhere. God sends to the pit those cities whose institutions produce such injurious individuals.

The dogs snarl and bite, and delight in confusion, and feed on offal. The inscription on their collar shows that they are a foreign breed.

The prophet affirms that by the sorceries of Babylon, all nations were deceived. The sorcery that exists here finds its nourishment elsewhere.

The statistics show that the murderers are from abroad, or, at least, that they are trained by outside influences. Those who incite men to murder by putting the bottle to their mouths, and making them drunk, are born in foreign lands. Those murderous nations which delight in war are not the Anglo-Saxons. They love peace.

Speaking of apostate Rome, the prophet declares that "She did corrupt the earth with her fornication." The symbolical fornication is nearly allied to the real. It is true that without are fornicators. De Tocqueville declares: " There is certainly no country in the world where the tie of marriage is more respected than in America, or where conjugal happiness is more highly or worthily appreciated."

Idolatry is cherished not here, but in pagan countries, and in great Babylon, or the apostate church, which is full of idols.

Those who love and make a lie, can be traced to that corrupt church, the characteristic of which, according to the apostle, is that of " speaking lies in hypocrisy." The Teutonic Christians are truth-loving.

One thing which has greatly aided in making our people strong and wise, is the fact that they have ever listened with attention to monitory words like these in Ezek. xxxiii:13: " When I say to the righteous, that he shall surely live; if he trust to his own righteousness, and commit iniquity, all his righteousness shall not be remembered; but for his iniquity that he hath committed, he shall die for it."

We shall never adequately prize our institutions till we know what the Lord has said about them. If we understand the prophecies in regard to the city of God, it will enliven our zeal and love for it. The best patriots love the Bible.

The prophet was made glad when he heard this useful prophecy. Just before Christ ascended, he made a promise to John, which he must have interpreted as meaning that he should have a long life, and that he should live till the Master came. Christ came to Patmos, and John heard his voice, and saw his face.

THE END.

CPSIA information can be obtained
at www.ICGtesting.com
Printed in the USA
LVOW10s0031110717

540827LV00035B/1592/P